INSIDE AMY

*Adults and Eating Disorders
Out in the Open*

Memoir of Anorexia Nervosa

by
LeAnne Brogan

PublishAmerica
Baltimore

ISBN: 1-4137-8744-4
PUBLISHED BY PUBLISHAMERICA, LLLP
www.publishamerica.com
Baltimore

Printed in the United States of America

Dedication

For my husband Jer, and my sons, Jerry and Sean.
I am blessed.

ACKNOWLEDGEMENTS

Essential to myself, LeAnne Brogan, I need to thank the loving individuals that have touched my life. Before anyone else, I thank my father and mother, for lovingly creating me in the eyes of God. My parents raised my six siblings and me in the best way that they knew how, back in the '50s, '60s and '70s. They worked hard their entire lives for us, provided for and nurtured us.

My mother was passive, reformed and overly protected as a child, and was very compliant to her husband's needs and wants, always before her own. I never heard my mother utter any abusive or offensive language in her entire life. My mother always worried about something, her list was everlasting. My father was domineering, arrogant and sometimes insulting. He was a true perfectionist. Raising seven children was a grand fulfillment for them, a lifelong challenge, with endless sacrifices, endurances and worries. I understand now that they loved each one of us and were proud of us, however open emotion was rarely displayed.

I have inherited many fine qualities and attributions, creativity, honesty and compassion from my parents. My mother once told me that I was "thrifty" like my Aunt Ann, my father's only sister, in California. I can extract the last drop of ketchup, jelly, or mayonnaise from its container, which shows the "never waste anything," side of me. My first-born relayed to me one day that he knows that I eat the "dust" from the bottom of a cereal box. My second born still gets one-half glass of a beverage to drink. "I'm not four years old Mom," he'll say to me. I recycle greeting cards into bookmarks, never purchase designer note cubes or notepads, and a bottle of shampoo can last a number of months for me. And I always save new clothes "for good." I cannot tell a lie and my children's continual inner presence grants me the genuine gifts of pride, empathy, trust, sincerity and a love for life.

My father's style of discipline, like many parents of that time was physical. He spanked or slapped his children, and his sarcasm and remarks were verbally abusive. I was always afraid of my father. It wasn't until he was diagnosed with cancer, in 1977, that I really began to understand him, learned to like, and then to love him. I realized then, that he loved me too. I do not place one ounce of blame on my parents for my eating disorder, "IT" (anorexia nervosa) created itself, within myself, as a protective mechanism. I loved my mother and father and finally was capable of telling them so, in my adult years. My parents, I love, honor, respect, and miss them.

I thank my siblings, Cathy, Jack, Rebecca, Tom, Mark and Bryan, and their extended families, for their support and love during my hospitalization in 1990 and the years that followed. I always felt proud when I relayed to other individuals that I came from a family of seven. A family that size is seldom seen today. Therapeutic treatment transformed my "withheld emotional feelings" closer to the surface, eventually expelling them outside, as I continue to write today. As a child, I always had someone to play with, or fight with, and we molded and bonded in special ways, we seven.

Thank you Theresa, my mentor, my second mom, for opening your heart and taking me under your wing. You always stopped whatever you were doing when I came to visit, and made special time just for me. With four children of your own, a husband and a home, the time in my life in the late '70s that I met and worked with you, I shall always cherish.

A special thank you to Rose and Rita, my stay-at-home-mom friends, after my first son was born. You accepted me, did not question me, and were always there when I needed you. My depression was severe, and when I mustered enough courage to come and visit, those times were helpful to me to get away from my seclusion.

To the entire professional faculty and staff of the Graduate

Hospital Eating Disorder Unit, especially Dr. Michael Pertschuk, Program Director, and the residents on the 20th floor of the Windsor Hotel, my thirty-day family, thank you.

Thank you ANAD, National Association of Anorexia Nervosa and Associated Disorders, Box 7, Highland Park, IL 60035, (847) 831-3438, www.anad.org for accepting me as a resource person to educate our youth more extensively about the dangers of eating disorders; and especially to President Vivian Hanson Meehan for writing the introduction to my book. A heartfelt blessing to each of the women I talk to daily on the ANAD support network website. You know who you are.

To the Administration, faculty, staff and volunteers affiliated within the Hazleton Area School District, especially the students, thank you. My hesitation and questioning of the decision to accept a full-time position outside of my hometown school, my thanks to Mrs. Jorgensen for her positive words, "LeAnne," "You can make it work."

To Mr. And Mrs. Joseph Gans, thank you for entering my life. Pat and Joe instilled confidence, trust, and ingenuine certitude toward my capability and credentials as an enabler to your son, Joseph. And to Joseph Gans V, "The Lion King," thank you for unveiling and entrusting your world to me.

Thank you Cath and Dr. Deb, for you were the first two individuals to read my unedited, handwritten manuscript. Thank you, Father Joseph Sica, for your unguided intrinsic gifts of honesty, optimism and positive words of encouragement toward my life adventure through telephone, the technology of e-mail and the opportunity to meet you in person in the chapel at Mercy Hospital, Wilkes-Barre, PA, after your Sunday mass.

Many thanks to Tamar Love Grande, my "cranky editor" in California, for giving me the opportunity to share my work with you and by adding your specialized qualities within my personal life story.

To Virginia and Kevin at Drums Elementary / Middle School, thank you for opening your heart and mind to my questions and concerns in regards to my manuscript. You never placed judgment upon me, nor looked at me as if I were a bizarre person with an eating disorder. You accepted me for who I have become and I honestly and thankfully say that I am finally content with who I am today. Thank you Ms. Turri, for giving me the opportunity to begin my speaking experience about eating disorders within your 7th grade classrooms. You welcomed me and elevated my confidence to continue my quest.

Thank you to Victor Beazzo, for recreating my vision of peacefulness, on the edge of the dock by the lake. Your artistic gift has captured the essence for my book's cover.

A special thank you to Attorney Donald G. Karpowich, for your professional courtesy in reviewing my legal material, and for your endless patience with my questions and concerns.

I thank God for the creation of my faithful canine companion, Abbey, my Little League girl. She listens when I need to vent my emotions and excitedly welcomes my arrival each time I enter my home.

I would like to acknowledge a few of the exceptional children I have worked with in school. Twins, Marley and Marissa, Michael, Joseph, Randy, Cassidy, David and Elizabeth, Charles, Brianna, Patrick and Maurice, Chloe, Mitchell, Zoe, Vincent, Christian, and Sean. What would we do without kids?

Finally and ultimately, thank you to my husband Jerry and my sons Jerry Jr. and Sean. As my emotions transpired throughout my written work, I inscribed my endless love for you. May God Bless Us and Keep Us in the Favor of His Loving Care.

I have made my lifelong Academy Award speech. I may now give myself a pat on the back, thumbs up, three cheers, and a hip-hip-hoorah! I survived my eating disorder!   Endlessly, out in the open, Inside Amy (LeAnne)   InsideAmy@hotmail.com

Contents

Introduction   11
Sibling Five of Seven   15
Amy's Sisters and Brothers   25
High School and James   34
Lake Beverly   43
United in Marriage   47
Firstborn Son   54
Shutdown and Hospitalization   64
The Graduate Hospital   72
Black Friday Breakthrough   78
Homecoming   90
Return to the Working World   98
Memories and a New Life   106
Welcome, Shawn   117
Amy's Mother   126
Life Goes On   135
Schoolchildren   142
Joseph and the Library   148
Her Place and Her Peace   161
In the End   173
Anorexia Nervosa   175

Introduction

LeAnne Brogan's book *Inside Amy* is a frank exposition of her long and courageous battle with anorexia nervosa, a deadly illness that nearly destroyed her, and her ultimate recovery. She describes in detail how the onset can occur as an adult. LeAnne's story is a message of hope that no matter how difficult, it is possible to overcome this pernicious illness and grow into a healthy and productive person.

She demonstrates her commitment to assist and educate others about the dangers of eating disorders through her volunteer efforts and serving as an ANAD (National Association of Anorexia Nervosa and Associated Disorders) Resource Person.

She faithfully describes the rise of negative thinking and feelings of unworthiness that are inherent to an eating disorder. The story provides insights into the importance of feelings to the development and maintenance of an eating disorder. Described, too, is the need for self-containment and self-sufficiency that restrains one's ability to ask for needed assistance and frequently to limit the assistance once treatment has been entered.

There are many women who develop an eating disorder later in life. The careful description of Amy from childhood to adulthood reveals that for some of these women an eating disorder is a problem waiting to happen. The characteristics of Amy's hidden anxieties caused by events beyond her control, accepting blame for such events, feeling unloved and therefore unworthy, feeling both invisible and wanting more invisibility to spare her from the wrath of her father. In the grips of occasional alcohol use a parent can vent rage felt over insufficiencies in his own life while "teaching" a child the consequences (through physical abuse or sarcastic put-downs) of disobeying his rules. Being inattentive, getting poor grades, being disrespectful, or showing poor judgment or impulse control when exploring behavioral boundaries could justify such "discipline".

Amy's mother was also a major target for her father's abuse. The demands of seven children plus verbal abuse led Amy's overwhelmed mother into negativity and depression. She was unable to provide the warmth and joy of being which Amy needed.

Amy was sensitive both to the dangers of displeasing her father and increasing the burden for her mother. She was, therefore, never able to voice her concerns to ask for either denial or confirmation of fears concerning the love for herself by her parents. She tried to be the perfect daughter. Improvements in her relationship with her father prior to his illness and death were not enough to allow her to accept herself fully.

She was fortunate that her childhood sweetheart from high school remained a constant in her life. In spite of this, her childhood perceptions and the low self-esteem engendered grew into exorbitant demands on her husband and his needs and threatened their peace together. Her husband's constancy never wavered. The birth of her son added complications, in part because of his physical problems not in her control and in part because she blamed herself for all problems.

After her father's death, her mother's needs became paramount to her. Amy gave and gave to be worthy of love. Amy did not talk about her feelings, but her actions continued to be bids for the love she perceived was never hers and an apology for her imperfections.

When these ministrations to others failed to fill her needs, she isolated more and more, smoked more, sewed more, controlled food more. Starvation provided the control that she was unable to envision through any other activity in her life. This control was the only accomplishment that gave her satisfaction. This was life's greatest satisfaction! Amy lived with the agony and this paltry reward for years before she was able to admit her life was unmanageable. She asked for help and allowed herself to be hospitalized for anorexia nervosa.

Amy is a classic example of the inability of an individual with an eating disorder to see the timely need for treatment. Even after the realization materializes and treatment is accepted, many do not see supportive treatment as an ongoing need—and so it was with Amy. Her story explains how unresolved emotions of the past trample on an individual's well-being over and over again until that person is unable to honor her/his worth and take from life what others take for granted. It tells us why the recovery journey is often so long and relapse part of the experience.

Amy's history is not unusual among those whose eating disorders appear in their 30's, 40's, or 50's but is not the only route for this process to occur. There are people without such childhood experiences who as adults suffer rejection, abuse, and loss after loss and finally succumb to eating disordered attitudes and behaviors. Unless life-affirming coping skills are learned, this can evolve into a full-blown eating disorder.

One of Amy's strengths lay in recognizing the benefits of change and after making the change accepting the potential for growth inherent in that change.

As a bystander, I rejoice in Amy's growth. A friend or relative might rejoice but cringe internally and say, "Why did it take so long?"

Why all the miserable years to realize yourself as a beautiful, deserving person? The only answer seems to be that treatment is a process and each demon of self-abnegation must be fought in turn. To those who succeed we must say, "Right on!"

Vivian Hanson Meehan
Founder and President
ANAD—National Association of Anorexia Nervosa and
Associated Disorders

Sibling Five of Seven

Twelve years ago, Amy told herself and her husband that when she turned 45, she would be gone. It was her goal, at that time in her life, to live at least that long. She was mid-life, hoping to finish the wondering, the floundering and the uncertainty of her 44 years, but she had secrets, many unveiled secrets, all bottled inside.

One evening, Amy's husband suggested that she should write a book. In her self-destructive mind, she thought, "Who would listen to *me*? Who would want to hear or care about *my* inner struggle?" In one year's time, she reconsidered and began to write. If she could not help others, perhaps she could finally help herself.

Amy was sibling number five, from a family of seven. She often thought that her parents should have stopped after their first two children. Her mother had always stated the exact order of her offspring: girl, boy, girl, boy, girl, boy, boy.

"Joseph should have been a little girl," her mother would say. "If he had, the sequence would have been perfect. Now, it's out of order." This was only one of many negative phrases her mother would repeat—a deeply depressed woman, her mother. The rest of the family seemed somewhat dysfunctional, as well. Amy's father never did anything "wrong"—just her mother and the rest of the family.

In Amy's home there was an unwritten rule, to be seen and not to be heard. Her father's standards were top shelf, first rate, the absolute best and the picture of perfection. Not one child would ever get there, thus, you were never good enough. Report card grades less than an A resulted in demeaning remarks. Household chores or daily responsibilities had to be flawless. If curfews were not met, if any sibling disobeyed his rules or ever tried to rebel, silence and ignorance was rendered to them. Oftentimes, spanking, or the use of his belt was the method of discipline. Amy feared the thought of being spanked by her father. Nightmares invaded her sleep.

As she grew up, Amy remembered very little. She was so afraid all of the time that she blocked out most of her early childhood and adolescent years. Blocked out, or blocked in.

In—inside, invisible, make not a sound, quiet and unnoticed—was how she existed. After Ann and John were born, there was less and less love and attention to go around. Susan, then Eric, Amy, Matthew and Joseph, the last in the line-up. Ah Joseph, the favorite! Amy's mother was 42 years old when he was born, delighted with him; even out of sequence, she loved, pampered and spoiled him. How proud her parents were of him! How Amy wanted to belong, to be loved, to matter to someone.

Shy and reserved as a child, her left thumb for comfort, Amy loved to rock in her rocking chair. She rocked and hummed. The quiet one, the good little girl, so afraid to speak for fear she'd receive that "look" from her father. Living in fear of the degrading remarks, the rejection, the humiliation and the verbal abuse she so frequently heard from her father, to each and every one of his children, even his wife. He rarely spoke a compliment; Amy never learned how to accept one.

Amy and her family lived in a small, coal-mining town in Northeastern Pennsylvania. Within each block in town were many homes, the area abundant with small children. She had many friends around her: Annie, Beth, Barbara, Janice and Laurie. They played simple childhood games, hopscotch, jump rope, hide and seek and dress-up, board games, card games and Barbie dolls. Amy recalled how the girls gathered on her open front porch one gloomy, rainy afternoon. She'd pull out the Ouiji board game. The girls giggled and rambled about the questions they asked the game about boys they had crushes on. Questions were about love, marriage and children. Strangely they were inquisitive about séances. Their young imaginations conjured up spiritual visitations from the dead. They'd chant in eerie voices that usually ended with shrieking and screaming. Amy appeared normal as a child.

Each Sunday, she and her brothers and sisters packed into the station wagon and went for a family drive. Another destination might have been set, to her grandmother's house, to a nearby farm to purchase sweet corn or apples, or a local amusement park, but they usually visited their great uncle's cabin near a small lake. One Sunday, in particular, Amy vividly remembered that her father pulled out of the driveway, her mother, brothers and sisters in the car, and left her behind. The good, quiet little girl, Amy played in her backyard, so silent, so timid, that no one missed her. They drove around the block before they realized they had forgotten her. Her family made light about the situation. Amy felt abandoned.

As a child, Amy formed a distinctive devotion to animals. When she was five years old, her family went to the Philadelphia Zoo. A photograph revealed her, with five of her siblings, alongside their mother, as they rested for a brief time to enjoy an ice-cream cone. There, she discovered her favorite animal, the polar bear. A towering, dominant, magnificent white bear! White meant purity, and the bear was so very powerful. Amy was pure, she felt, but not powerful. Her skin was fair, her hair as light as the sunshine. Bashful, timid, sensitive, barely visible—she used that word, "invisible." Polar bears exhibited a mighty strength, strength for which she yearned. Anxiety, anger and fear welled up inside her, day after day. She experienced these feelings, unaware of what they were. She kept them inside, deep within her, for days, weeks, months, and years...

Amy's father worked long hours in a local, clothing manufacturing company. He was employed as a a machinist and a mechanic. She remembered the rows upon rows of sewing machines, each faced by a woman intently sewing shirts, jackets and coats. Bolts of fabric were everywhere. Her father maintained the proper operation of the machines. This was his job, a paycheck to support his family. He disliked the continual badgering of the women employed there, the stress and the overtime. It certainly was not a very fulfilling occupation for him, nor did he receive any appreciation from his employers, for all his hard work.

Exactly ten minutes before his arrival from the factory, Mrs. Montgomery alerted the children that their father was coming. It was time to be quiet and respectful. Their father had worked hard all day long and he deserved a quiet atmosphere. He came home exhausted, hungry and angry. Six children were there to greet him at the end of each day. He showed little, if any, affection or attention toward them. As he looked down upon them, the children were expected to be quiet when he wanted to watch television, read the newspaper or listen to the stereo. He smoked a pipe or cigarettes, and sometimes he drank in excess.

When he became intoxicated, Amy was even more afraid of him. She was terrified of him! Her mother was upset with him in that condition, too, but never voiced her opinion or showed her feelings. His anger toward his wife and children escalated. He became belligerent and obnoxious. Later in her life, Amy realized that there was a name to that type of mistreatment: verbal abuse. Instead of vitamins, she and her siblings received daily doses of verbal abuse. "For cryin' out loud, can't you do anything right?" he'd holler. "Good gravy!" "Hold the flashlight where I can see!" "You do what you are told to do, or you'll be grounded for a week!" "If you misbehave, I'll send you kids to Kislin!" (Kislin was the name for a detention home) "You'll never amount to anything."

"Mark my words." Oh, never mind, I'll do it myself!" These were just a sample of some of her father's expressions.

Amy even sensed how fearful her own mother was of her husband, which made Amy feel very unstable and unprotected. Who was there for support, for comfort, for love? When her father raised his voice and became angry with her mother, Amy's response was to protect her mother. They were never, ever allowed to show any true feelings. If they did, the greatest fear of all happened. His temper heightened, his voice became louder. His right arm rose. Would he dare strike one of them? Would he strike her mother? Amy's heart and soul felt the terror. She simply kept her feelings inside.

The most unsettling times were at meals. As a family, they gathered around a large, rustic, picnic-style pine table. Her mother was an excellent cook and baker. At most meals, though, her father had a nasty and degrading comment about the preparation or taste of the food. Her mother felt so terrible. She would apologize to him, and sometimes she even excused herself from the dinner table, while the children sat, watching. Amy was extremely uncomfortable. She wanted to crawl underneath the table, her appetite destroyed. All she wanted to do was to run and help her mother, but she knew it was better to sit in front of her untouched plate until her father excused them.

At holiday gatherings, especially Thanksgiving, the tension at the dinner table heightened. At every blessed Thanksgiving, her father insulted the meal's taste, her mother began to despise preparing the turkey. It was always too dry. With this much anxiety, how could the family be thankful?

Amy spoke not a word. She programmed her feelings inward. Her father left the table for a smoke or a drink, even to visit his brother's home, never to spend much time with his own family. Each holiday, each special occasion, came and departed, all the same. To this day, Amy and at least two of her siblings have difficulty spending time gathered at a dinner table.

Amy grew up in the Roman Catholic faith. Her family was avid members of St. John's Nepomocene Roman Catholic Church. A huge, majestic, stone structure, it was built in the early 1900's, strategically located on the corner of South and Vine. When the children entered the second grade, around eight years of age, they received First Holy Communion—Sunday mass and Holy Days of Obligation, sacraments to fulfill, traditions and customs, abstinence and fasting, all strictly followed.

Rules of the church were similar to the rules of the house, obey, or you were overlooked, ignored, and punished. The children had to be properly dressed; the girls were required to wear white veils on the top of their heads, held securely with a bobby pin. Once inside the church, there was complete silence. If someone dared to whisper, the parishioners gaped. Amy felt as though God would punish her, by disturbing His presence. She was unsafe and frightened at home, and oftentimes felt the same way about her faith in God and Sunday mass.

She recalled the organ music, the choir, and the women who prayed the rosary each week before mass began. They were so repetitive and depressing. It was all so depressing.

There was a black-and-white photograph of Amy, in her white, taffeta Communion dress, as she stood in her backyard. A beaded veil adorned her head, her hands clasped in a prayer-like manner, her head lowered in shame, tears gently rolling down her face. Why? Why was she crying? She felt embarrassed and self-conscious, as though she had done something wrong. She stood before her father and mother, her father behind the camera. That feeling that emulated from her father's presence…why should he take a picture of her? She could not understand. She was not worthy of a compliment, shunned them, so why were they taking her picture? Were they proud of her for some reason? She just wanted to disappear.

In fourth grade, something happened, a piece of an intricate puzzle laid into place.

Her mother was angry because Amy was late for supper. Amy had enjoyed a game of dodgeball after school with her friends. It was a Tuesday, her mother's night out for bowling, as Wednesday was canasta with her card-club friends. Amy ate her late dinner, under her mother's contemptuous glare, fully aware of her discontent. Her mother departed for the bowling alley. Amy finished homework and sat to watch television with her two brothers and her father. In the evening, when her father relaxed, he usually had the news, a documentary, a *National Geographic* special or *Wild Kingdom* on the set. On this particular evening, the show was about animals and their offspring, the birth, nurturing and instinctive qualities of various species. As Amy watched a litter of puppies being born, she suddenly felt awkwardly ill. As she leaned forward in her seat, she vomited on the floor. Her father grabbed a basin, and she became ill again.

From that moment on, Amy had a severe phobia, an intense fear of vomiting. If someone were about to vomit or choke, or if someone simply had a distressing cough, it sent Amy into a panic. She became immobilized. She always wondered why these episodes occurred. Were they related to her mother's anger with her? Was it the absolute fear of her father and the fact that he had to take care of her that night? It must have been a bother to him. Amy remembered how frightened she was to ask if she could stay with her mother that night, after Amy's mother came home from bowling. Bits and pieces were taking shape; a troubled young girl had begun to evolve.

Transition into puberty and adolescence was an awkward time for Amy, as it is for most children. Amy mustered all the courage within her to ask her mother about menstruation, to purchase proper underclothing for her and to have permission to attend the sixth-grade dance.

She visualized that evening. Amy had been taking a bath as her mother applied make-up by the bathroom mirror. Out of sight, Amy felt less jittery presenting these concerns. "Mom", she said, "some of the girls in my class have started to get their periods, wear bras, and talk about boys and how they have begun to look at us. And do you think I could go to the dance?" she quickly added. Amy took a deep breath, relieved that she had gotten it out. "Yes," her mother replied. "We can go to Raccasin's tomorrow to buy what you need. Everything was trying, especially asking her parents for things.

She felt she deserved the excruciating cramps and nausea that arrived each month when her period began. She cried with the pain and discomfort and held tightly to a heating pad. Every month, for the first two days, she ate very little food. Chicken noodle cup-a-soup, crackers and hot tea usually helped. Years went by before she asked her mother if there was anything a doctor could prescribe for her to relieve the pain. It simply did not occur to her that the pain could go away; that there was something she could do to relieve her agony.

Junior high school, grades six through eight, and the youngest of the siblings was born. Joseph and Amy had ten years between them, twenty years between he and Ann.. Shortly after his birth, their grandparents on their mother's side passed on. Baba and Joe Joe, Amy had lovingly called them. Amy's mother descended into a deeper depressive state.

As Amy approached her teen-aged years, her sense of self-worth and stability began to decline even further. Amy identified subtle changes within her during these years. A very young girl who needed support and guidance, positive direction and undivided attention, Amy became dysfunctional, confused and uncertain.

When she gathered with friends to sun and swim—achieving a tan was quite the "in" thing to do—Amy always burned under the rays of the sun because of her fair skin. But sunburn was an accomplishment for her. She'd turn beet red, blister, and experience chills and endure pain all over her body. Perhaps, she thought, if her symptoms were severe enough, someone might notice her. She began, at certain times, to experience episodes of shakiness, a sort of nervousness. "The shakes" she'd call them. Unable to predict their onset, she trembled uncontrollably at odd times throughout the day. She'd clench her teeth to control her jaw and teeth from chattering, never telling anyone about these episodes, of course. She taught herself how to deal with obstacles, alone.

Normal teenaged milestones came and went: braces and boyfriends, cliques and sleepovers. Childhood memories were vague and distant. She never had friends stay overnight; she was afraid to ask permission. Her cousin, Cindy had the gang over on Friday nights. Her father always made his special recipe pizza. All the girls loved it! Her mother was jaunty and easygoing and was interested in the girl talk. Amy envied her cousin's popularity and her outward disposition. At Cindy's, it was laughter and party time!

Another friend was Laurie. She lived in a small ranch house on Crescents Road, with a vast backyard, where they practiced gymnastics and cheerleading routines. A very unique area between her house and the forest were rows of red raspberry bushes. How they loved to pick the fruit when it was ripe! Amy always took a container home to share with her mother. With Laurie, Amy envied the relationship she had with her parents. They were so polite and pleasant, and Amy noticed how they kissed their daughter on the forehead whenever she was going out somewhere.

Negative events outweighed the positive. The majority of Amy's siblings were older than she was. Each sibling coped differently within the family, some more destructive than others. All were quite athletic, involved in basketball, baseball, softball and cheerleading. Ann loved to read, novel after novel. Eric constructed model cars and airplanes, and excelled in cross-country. Amy had a love for gymnastics, music, and coloring and using her Spirograph for drawing. She began to develop a strong desire for perfection. Matthew played quietly with Matchbox cars and a racetrack.

Amy loved her brothers and sisters; however, she could not communicate with them. Their relationships had no bond or closeness, no genuine feeling of love. When they gathered together, Amy wanted to hide, to disappear. What would they talk about? She felt afraid, afraid to be with her own family. She didn't fit in. She felt inferior to them. Her siblings, especially those who attended college, were somehow better than her, Amy thought.

There were Christmas parties and Easter egg hunts. Mr. Montgomery was a member of a community organization called the Elks. Every year they held a Christmas party for the member's children. Amy remembered hot dogs and potato chips and cookies. Every child received a new toy.

There was a little hardware store on Centre Street called Bonomo's. In the springtime, usually around the Easter holiday, they sold live bunnies and chicks and displayed them in the front window of the store for all passersby to see. Amy remembered receiving a bunny when she was seven or eight years old. She and Matthew took care of it. Occasionally, the family made reservations to go out to dinner at a restaurant. Oddly, she loved to order turkey, mashed potatoes and gravy with a vegetable. Special occasions came and went, lacking true joy or happiness. Always present was the feeling of tension and stress. On the outside, Amy was a frivolous, whimsical girl, and on the inside, she was always afraid, always wary. She began to display two sides of herself.

Amy's Sisters and Brothers

In 1968, Amy was ten years old. Her eldest sister, Ann, and brother, John, were already in college when their youngest sibling, Bryan was born. Susan and Eric were in high school, Matthew and she in elementary. Daniel Coxe Memorial was the name of her school, DCM for short. It was a two-story high, solid brick structure, built on the corner of Washington and Chestnut Streets. She remembered her sister Susan walked her to school. Amy cried every day. Off to the cloakroom she'd go, tissue in hand, afraid of being separated from her mother.

Easter holidays seemed the most comfortable to bear, as Our Lord and Savior rose on the third day, entering into the Kingdom of Heaven. Her mother prepared ham and kielbasa, red beets with horseradish, paska bread, and the traditional scrambled egg and milk, ball-shaped mixture called citic or hrutka, in Slavish. The siblings gathered to dye hard-boiled eggs at the kitchen table. Amy's mother prepared nut and poppy seed rolls, a favorite of their mothers baking. The Easter bunny brought chocolate treats to each and every one of them. Chocolate candy on Easter morning! What a rare and special treat!

Simply describing Amy's family began with Ann, a straight-A student; she pursued Bachelor's and Master's degrees in secondary education, majoring in English, at Bloomsburg University. She became an English teacher and met her future husband, Bill, a secondary education math major. He received his Bachelor's degree and Master's equivalency in Education, and they wed in August of 1971.

Ann and Bill had a major religious conflict: Ann's family was of the Roman Catholic faith, and Bill's was Protestant. Theirs was not a proper "match," according to the rules and regulations of Catholic beliefs. Imagine her parents' dismay and disappointment when Ann and Bill announced their engagement. To her parents, this was an imperfection. Their first-born had failed to conform to the rules of Catholicism. They were angry and upset, to say the least. What would the neighbors think, and the folks at the factory?

Amy's family's church was the largest, most majestic in their small town. Within the structure were exquisite stained-glass windows, inviolable statues and an impressive, balcony-established organ, all vivid in Amy's mind. After her mother and father had passed away, Amy had extreme difficulty attending masses in that church.

Bill and Ann, completely aware of her parent's unhappiness, rose beyond it with their love for one another. They were blessed with three wonderful children and gave a promise, a commitment, that their children would be raised in the Roman Catholic faith. Bill was to follow the sacraments, First Penance, First Holy Communion and Confirmation. He practiced weekly Catechetical classes and prayers, novenas and rosaries, and he followed the teachings of the Ten Commandments, a mere handful of Catholic traditions that would now become Bill's traditions. All three children were baptized, but only their eldest daughter received the Sacraments of Communion and Confirmation.

Torn between her love for her parents and her love for her own family, Ann and her children stopped attending St. John's Roman Catholic Church. After her father passed away in 1987, Ann left the Catholic Church and joined her husband's family church. This was the right decision for Ann, who finally felt comfortable and at peace within herself. Ann was a strong woman. Amy loved and admired her eldest sister, and sheltered her from their parents' harsh words.

John, Amy's big brother, was second in line of eldest to youngest. Tall, lean, handsome and athletic, he graduated from Mansfield State College with a degree in special education. He took up residence in Pittsburgh with his wife, Mary, and their two beautiful daughters.

Despite John's success, Amy's father seemed disappointed in his son. Somehow, none of the children ever lived up to his expectations—his expectations of perfection, Amy presumed.

When he was younger, John dabbled with cigarettes and alcohol in his teen and college years, during the early 1970s. Hippies, peace and love, bell-bottoms and long hair prevailed. The Vietnam War had begun, but John avoided it by going to college. After he graduated, he moved to a quaint, little town named Ebensburg, Pennsylvania, and began his career as a Special Education teacher. He and Mary, also a teacher, were married in 1978. In addition to their teaching positions, they opened a small, retail-clothing store, selling merchandise from his father's manufacturing company, back home. The business did well for them, due in part to John's ambition and incredible stamina. Tragically and unexpectedly, after a few short years, his place of business burned down. Amy never really knew how it actually happened and was afraid to ask. Imagining how upset they must have been, she could not approach those feelings of sadness and despair. She wanted to reach out to her brother and console him, but she did not know how.

Not only did John feel displaced within his own family, but he also had to prove his proficiency with his in-laws, as well. Prove it he did: he bounced back from his company's loss and he continued to succeed, pursuing his post-graduate education. In 1985, he received his Master's degree in Special Education; a few years later, he took his Doctoral Degree in Education Administration and Leadership Studies.

Amy was so proud of her brother! She wished that someone could be proud of her, that she could do something, anything, to earn someone's pride. Subconsciously, she continued to believe in the idealistic atmosphere of perfection that surrounded her. Perfection, flawlessness and impeccability—these were the keys to earning acceptance and affection. She knew she possessed none of these qualities.

Susan was third-born, strong-willed, perseverant and liberated. A tomboy as a child, Susan's friends were the boys in the neighborhood. She was eager to participate in any active game; baseball and basketball were her favorites. Back in the 60's, women were not prevalent participants in sports, but Susan had her heart set to play Little League baseball. Susan was Hall of Fame material; however, she was never given the opportunity to try. Girls were simply not allowed to play back then.

One day in the backyard, her sister hit a home run that smashed the baseball through their neighbor, Mr. Oleander's, window. Their mother said, "Wait until your father gets home!" Immediately, Amy was filled with anxiety and fear for the remainder of the day until finally 3:30 arrived. When their father found out what Susan had done, he grabbed her by the arm, spanked her and sent her to her room. Amy witnessed it all. Sometimes their father used his belt when he spanked them, and sometimes just his hand. Had he hit all his children? She could not remember.

In Susan's high school basketball career, she averaged 25 points per game. For three consecutive years, she led the Girl's League as the highest scorer. She was chosen each year for the All-Star Team. And yet recognition of her athletic prowess went unnoticed. The female team members never received a trophy, jacket, plaque or letter, despite their accomplishments. Amy did not realize how much this oversight had upset her sister until they grew older. When women's liberation highlighted the 70s, only then did change occur.

Amy admired the girl's softball team that her sister played on. Susan's had such style and ability whenever Amy watched her hit and pitch. Susan guided Amy when she was old enough to join the league, but Amy wished she had even one-quarter of her sister's talent.

Susan and Amy shared the attic bedroom, which Susan painted lavender. She had long, chestnut-colored hair, center parted and straight as a ruler. She wore jeans with a fringed belt and jacket. Amy thought she was very cool, and someday wanted to be like her.. When Susan went off to college, she invited Amy to join her one particular weekend and watch a gymnastics competition, a sport she knew Amy loved. Amy was thrilled Susan had taken time out for her.

Susan had no time whatsoever for dances, for frilly, feminine dresses or for boyfriends. In college, she became somewhat opposed to the opposite sex; the years of emotional abuse from her father directed her anger towards men. She was steadfast with her opinions and very forward and outspoken. As the years passed, Amy sensed her dislike for and disrespect of their father. Although she was always uncomfortable when her sister and brothers called him "the old man," she never breathed a word of it to them, of course.

Susan graduated with a Bachelor's degree in Physical Education and received her Masters degree in Psychology. She moved from the "Twilight Zone," as she nicknamed their little town, first to Massachusetts, and then to New Hampshire, and finally to Los Angeles. She resides there today. In 1991, Susan disclosed to Amy that she would remain a single woman and never have children. This was Susan's choice to be far removed from her father and her hometown. Amy accepted her decision. Susan was her sister, and she loved her, no matter what.

After Susan, Eric arrived. Whereas the eldest, John, resembled their father in appearance, Eric had similar personality traits. The closest in age to Amy, Eric and she shared a special bond, even though he displayed his affection in a teasing way at times: He would take the end of a towel, wet the tip of it, twist it and snap it at her. She loathed that snapping sound and the stinging feeling. He'd snicker, and she'd chase after him.

In high school, Eric played on the baseball and basketball teams and was very popular with his peers. At the tender age of 16, he began to smoke and party with his friends; in the 70s, laws weren't enforced as strictly as they were in later decades. Sporting a classic smirk when he grinned, Eric grew his hair to shoulder length, which his father detested. He often reprimanded Eric about it, and Eric became somewhat defiant.

When Eric became involved in troublesome situations, his mother protected him, keeping the truth hidden from her husband. Amy knew why. She wanted to protect her children from her husband's anger, the outrage, insults and language he used. Amy feared him, cringing at the sound of his voice.

An uptown teenage hangout, the Pool Room, was a forbidden place, where the boys shot a game of pool, purchased cigarettes or congregated with friends. Of course, Eric and his peers were drawn there. Amy vividly remembers the day when her father caught Eric in the Pool Room. She was on her way down from her room, on the stairway, when she heard awful shouting from outside the window. Amy crouched down on the stairs to peer between the stair posts, through the window. She first caught a glimpse of her brother, Eric, who was trying to protect himself from their father, who slapped Eric's face as they passed the window and entered the back door. Eric cringed and stumbled into the house. Amy wasn't certain how many times her father had struck Eric, but she saw blood coming from his nose and mouth. Their father continued to shout, and she quickly scrambled up the stairs, unseen, unheard. She was petrified, once again, of what she had seen. *Stop! Stop hitting my brother!* But she could only scream the words inside herself.

Amy's personality was shy and naive, simple, innocent, and honest. She could never speak badly against anyone, and certainly not her father! She was a good girl. She had to be! She had to be, or he might hate her, he might hurt her. She feared being stricken by him. She had to protect herself, her siblings and her mother. Unable to release her emotions, every minute glitch in her path of life became uncontrollable for her. Where her siblings accepted their parents' child-raising methods as a part of growing up, Amy perceived every circumstance as a personal failure, and felt she had to take care of everyone else's problems.

She wondered where everyone else was. Where was her mother? Would she be her father's next victim? Again, that awful, dreading feeling of terror filled her. It happened more frequently, anxiety, helplessness, and the apprehension of speaking. Who would protect her? Who would take care of Amy? She felt so lost and alone. She just wanted to disappear, stay hidden and become invisible.

Two years after Eric, Amy was born, and then Matthew. The elder siblings recalled her quiet and soothing nature and how she adored her rocking chair. With her thumb in her mouth, at times she rocked so forcefully that she banged her head. They may have thought it a bit unusual. To Amy, it was a coping mechanism .

A remote, quiet child, just like his sister, Amy, Matthew was next in the line up. He and Amy were often forgotten in the shuffle of siblings. Her memory groped for pits and pieces of their shared childhood. Matthew had little desire for sports and had an immense fear of water, a fear their mother instilled in Matthew, as well as in Amy. They were at the base of the totem pole; oftentimes, the elder siblings watched out for them.

Immediately after graduating from high school, Matthew moved out. He rented a small apartment in the Poconos and found employment in a restaurant as a head cook. For many years, alcohol, cigarettes and drugs were his only family. One Friday evening, a telephone call came for Amy's father. Matthew had overdosed, lost control and completely trashed his apartment. No one ever said a single word about the incident. Everything was always kept a secret.

He seldom stopped home to visit, and when he did, he was reclusive and very distant. On the few occasions that Matthew did come home, Amy was uncomfortable when she had to converse with him. He spoke only when someone spoke first to him. He never added other conversation to keep the momentum flowing. Amy felt squeamish in his presence. Matthew had the strength to leave the homestead and get a place of his own. Amy could not. She felt inferior to all of them.

Matthew married a woman named Janie and adopted her daughter, Dawn, who was eight years old at the time. Janie wanted and expected much more than Matthew offered her. After two years, they had a natural child together, named Heather, in the hope of saving their marriage. Heather was two when the marriage ended.

The divorce became unpleasant, and Amy found herself in the middle of the tension. She was sorry for her brother's failed marriage and for his troubled past. Everyone seemed to turn to Amy for support. She was the listener, the comforter and the healer. She gave all of herself to everyone, anyone, who needed help. She wanted to make things perfect for the people she loved and help all of those that touched her life, even if it meant sacrificing herself.

Joseph was the youngest of Amy's siblings, the last to be born, when Amy's parents were in their forties. Joseph was their miracle, their pride and joy! They were older and wiser now, so Amy's parents, brothers and sisters overwhelmed him with love and undivided attention. Joseph was the baby. Whatever he wanted, he received. He had the newest bicycle, name brand clothing, and the first videogame station, Atari. For years, Amy's mother did his homework for him when he didn't understand the material or simply was too lazy. He was accepted in the family. There was no anger, no disappointment and no disillusionment with him. Twenty years younger than Ann, he was three years old when she and Bill married.

In his infancy, roughly around eight months, Joseph had to be hospitalized. Their mother was deeply depressed after the sudden loss of her parents, and her home-life, husband and children all added to her depression and instability. Joseph suffered nutritionally and physically and showed signs of delayed development. Within a week, he was home again, with Susan and Amy helping out as much as they could. Their father worked overtime at the factory to make ends meet, and Amy's mother began a part-time job in a local bank as a teller, which led to a full-time position. The girls were caretakers for young Joseph.

The odd-numbered, seven siblings made quite a large family in comparison to today's families. The eldest three matured and went off to college, and two married. The middle threesome seemed merely to exist, and young Joseph prevailed.

Amy continued to conform into a compliant, submissive, amiable young girl. She tried hard to please, to keep everything in her life smooth, without controversy, without error. John, Susan and Eric entered rebellious phases with smoking and dabbling in alcohol with friends. Surprised by their actions, Amy never let on that she knew, or how bothered she felt about it. If her father found out, she did not want to be around for the consequences.

She was everyone's caretaker, even her mother's, while Amy's soul filled with her father's anger and criticism, her mother's chronic complaints, depression and failing health. Mrs. Montgomery was a pleasant woman while she worked in the bank. She needed the diversion and social aspects of her job and was admired by her friends. When the weekend arrived, everything went downhill. "Who will take me shopping? "How will I get to my doctor's appointment?" She hated to ask her children for help and felt as though she were a burden to her family. The children, including Amy, resented the way she made them feel. No matter how much everyone helped her out, she managed still to complain about something.

Whenever Amy experienced emotions that were too intense, she trapped them inside her, unaware of how to deal with them. She locked them inside, kept them a secret. She wanted to remain invisible, a ghost. A protective wall had begun to form around her.

High School and James

High school: The year was 1972 and Amy was a freshman in high school. She was a cheerleader, and a member of the school's gymnastics team, active in drama club and an aide in the school office. She felt she was a part of the popular group of girls her age. She fit in and was accepted by her peers. Practices, games and competitive meets kept her active and busy; summer camps and part-time jobs helped her grow and mature into a young lady. Subtle changes in her body were disturbing. She was unhappy with the acne that appeared on her face, and envied the girls who were flawless. Unsatisfied, as well with her body, she'd peer into a full-length mirror and see a flat-chested girl with a protruding belly. Why didn't she develop sensual curves like her friends did? They were far more attractive than she and caught the eyes of the boys. Would the opposite sex ever notice her?

In her sophomore year, October of 1973, members of the opposite sex began to take notice to her. One of her brother Eric's friends asked her out on her first date. He was a short, stout boy, not extremely attractive; nonetheless, Amy accepted. Always the good girl, she did not know how to say "no" to this boy, how to spare his feelings.

Back in those days, a date meant a cruise around town in a boy's car, if he had one, and then parking in a secluded area to be alone. Early in the evening, Amy felt awkward and wished that the night would come to an end; she could never let this boy know how she really felt. She hardly spoke a word to him the entire time, she was very afraid. She could not refuse his advances; he placed his hand on her back underneath her shirt. She did not know how to speak up for herself, and just say "No." She silently prayed to God that he would not touch her any further. He pulled out of the parking area at last and drove Amy home. When he stopped in front of her house to drop her off, she leaned over and kissed him, again simply to be pleasing and polite. She mentally rehearsed how she would let him know she did not want another date, and she managed to tell him in school—politely, of course—later that same week.

Two other boys her age expressed their interest in her, but she didn't accept dates from them. It wasn't until the third boy called, James, a neighbor that lived just two blocks from her house, that she accepted his offer for a night out at the local movie theater. The big date was set for a Friday evening in late December, and they met that night in front of the movie house.

Amy was excited and nervous. James was fifteen, handsome, tall and lean, and he played on the varsity basketball and baseball teams. From the beginning of the date, she was completely infatuated with him. She couldn't even remember what movie they saw! She only remembered that they sat in the balcony, and it was dark. After the movie, James walked her home. About a block from her house, he stopped on the corner. Amy thought at first that he did not know where she lived. Then he turned Amy toward him and ever so gently kissed her on her lips. She was taken by surprise, completely overwhelmed by that intimate moment. He grasped her hand, and they continued to walk to her doorstep. They said "good night" to one another, and she stepped inside. All night long, she thought of him and did not sleep at all.

They began a courtship or "going steady" relationship, as it was called, making them a regular item in their sophomore class. He was the ball player, and she the cheerleader. They and their friends would dash out of the YMCA gym after a basketball game to grab a booth at their favorite hangout restaurant, Dot's, where they usually ordered cheeseburgers, toasted ham-and-cheese sandwiches and french fries with gravy.

Oddly, Amy never ordered anything for herself. She felt that James should not spend his money on her, and that she did not deserve that kind of treat. No one should pay her special attention or compliment her. She just wasn't worthy of the attention. James always shared his meal with her, and she was beginning to feel as though he treated her in a special and caring manner—not at all how she was accustomed to being treated in her family.

It took Amy a good three months until she uttered more than a few words to Jim. He was the type of person that never had a loss for words. He talked about school and his participation with the golf and baseball teams. They were both in the school play and he'd ask if she knew her lines. James knew Amy's brother Eric and his friends very well. Sometimes they all hung out together. They went to the movies or shopping at the mall. He discovered how extremely shy Amy was and was determined to win her over. He truly loved her. Amy either shrugged her shoulders or simply responded with "I don't know." She was filled with 15 years of fear, a fear of her father that evolved into extreme nervousness around men. How could she trust this young man? Eventually, he would ridicule her or talk to her abusively. She'd been taught apprehensiveness and panic. She had to be cautious and wary, or she would crumble completely. What patience and endurance he showed for her!

One winter evening, after a basketball game, they huddled together in a doorway downtown. Their friends were gathered in groups, celebrating a sports victory over a top-notch team. James, ever so softly, whispered into Amy's ear, "I love you." She looked into his eyes, smiled at him, and they embraced. Amy did not know how to respond. She was astounded by his words. No one had ever said those words to her, that they loved her before. Not her parents, siblings, grandparents or her friends. In fact, she had never heard those three simple words. She realized she was falling in love with this boy!

From that moment on, all Amy wanted was to be with James. Every morning, she walked the block down to his house, knocked on the door, walked inside and sat on the bottom stair until he woke up for school. Hand in hand, and oftentimes arms around each other, they'd walk to class. In the evening they talked on the telephone, and saw each other a few nights a week. They sat together on the school bus when they traveled to games.

James soon got his drivers license and they began to cruise about their small town. There was a special place they frequented for an ice cream cone and usually a Mountain Dew or Dr. Pepper. James knew how Amy loved animals and always stopped at a fenced in area where two deer were looked after. Amy was prepared with apples and carrots to hand feed the pair. They were very special to her.

She hated to leave him when it came time to part and go back to their homes. He made her feel so very special. James placed Amy on a pedestal and treated her like a princess. They teased and laughed together, and looked ahead to their future .

Although they were happy, she began to feel difficult emotions. She was becoming possessive of him, easily angered and agitated when he went out with his friends. She needed to have him exclusively for herself. Feelings of jealousy and insecurity erupted. An obsession brewed. She slowly maneuvered her way into his bloodstream. In no time at all, they were phoning and seeing each other every day. They were head-over-heels in love with one another. She began to experience, for the first time, a slight feeling of control in the way she acted toward Jim. He loved her so much that he was always eager to do what she wanted.

The time came for them to meet each other's parents. Jim came from a loving, lighthearted, Irish Catholic family. His father was a retired postal carrier who loved to read, and his mother was a dominant, energetic hair stylist. Mrs. Bailey's beauty shop was on the second floor, and her faithful and longtime patrons climbed the stairs each week for their regular beautifying appointments. There was classic salon chitchat, gossip and laughter. Mr. Bailey spent most of his time in the kitchen, reading and having a few beers. Jim came from a large family, as well, with three brothers and two sisters.

Amy was much more comfortable when they spent time at Jim's home. The atmosphere there was so different than it was at Amy's house. There was happiness in that home. They cared for one another and shared with each other. Jim's mother was caring and nurturing, and his father was a passive, intellectual man. They welcomed Amy into their home and always tried to make her feel special.

Mrs. Bailey was an extremely religious woman, truly a saint. She taught Amy how to give from her heart, as well as to receive. In her bedroom closet, she had an array of beauty products, stationery, children's toys and books, to simply have on hand in case she needed a gift for someone. "How clever," Amy thought. "She always brought a smile to someone she loved." When a friend or family member was ill or hospitalized, she'd pray for them and always send a get-well card with a few Lottery rub-off tickets inside. If she had a house large enough, she'd invite the entire neighborhood for dinner. She had a heart of gold. There was always a kind word, a compliment and a prize, all expressions of love. Mrs. Bailey's manner was unique, very genuine.

In Jim's house, holidays were exorbitantly happy times. The family and relatives gathered, along with friends and neighbors. Mrs. Bailey spent weeks preparing for holidays and special occasions. At Christmas and Easter, she showered her children and grandchildren with so many gifts! Their home abounded with merriment and festivity. But the most jubilant day of the year for Mr. Bailey was St. Patrick's Day. He dressed in his finest green attire, a corsage pinned to his lapel and a green beret resting atop his head, and proudly marched in the town's annual parade.

Holidays in Amy's home were uneasy, unhappy times. Preparation meant tension. She anticipated her father's intoxicated state and his belligerent and abusive comments to her mother. There were no relatives, neighbors or friends at any celebration. Her mother complained about all the work she had to do, and she knew that however she had prepared, it would not meet her husband's expectations. When the time came for the family to sit down at the dinner table, Amy was restless and fearful.

Amy continued to fine-tune her "pleasing" characteristics. At Christmas, she tried to purchase or create the most impressive gift for her father that she could imagine. She thought that if he loved the gift, he would love her, too. Once, she purchased a white dolphin figurine, perfectly positioned on a piece of driftwood. Her father loved dolphins, actually any type of ocean fish or mammal. He had served in the navy in Hawaii during World War II, and often spoke of his experiences there. Another special gift was a family collage she put together and placed inside a carved oak frame. Amy spent weeks selecting just the right photographs for it. She thought she saw tears well up in his eyes that Christmas. "He must really like it," she thought.

As the years passed and holidays approached, Amy became overwhelmed with sadness. She dreaded any and every holiday. Any familiar music and songs of the season further depressed her.

She and James stayed together all throughout their high school years, very much in love. Graduation came in June of 1975, after which they started to work right away to save money so they could be married. Amy's parents had asked her about college, but she felt they could not afford to send her, so she declined. James found a job locally, at an automobile distributing company, and Amy accepted a job in a factory that manufactured aircraft transformers.

Amy soon found out that assembly labor was not an enjoyable occupation, nor were the women she worked with pleasant or friendly. Most of the women were married, with children, and were very unhappy with their lives. They gossiped and complained for most of the shift, especially about their husbands. Every night, Amy looked forward to having James to cling to, but the job took its toll on her. She began to feel unconditionally sad. First her home life, and then her workdays, left her feeling unfulfilled. At the day's end, she wept.

Of all the women she worked with at the factory, one very special person entered Amy's life. Her name was Theresa. She took Amy under her wing, like a mother bird, making time for her. Amy could reveal her deepest secrets and her darkest fears to Theresa, often Amy visiting her at home, where they talked for hours. Amy met Theresa's husband and four children. A wife and mother, age 35, bonded with a young woman, age 17. Another human being, Amy discovered, had shown her love and attention. Theresa listened and was a genuine friend, a mentor. She entered Amy's heart and forever held a place there.

After two years of factory life, Amy's mother searched the newspaper ads and showed Amy a receptionist/assistant position listed for a local dental office. The ad said "no experience necessary" and offered on the job training. Mrs. Montgomery knew the dentist and his family. She offered advice to her daughter on what outfit to wear for her interview, and a few pointers for answering questions. Amy applied for it and landed the job. She was delighted and felt confident that she could train for the position. Most important, she felt positive about the one-on-one work atmosphere in the dental office. Each day was a new challenge and learning experience for her.

When Amy was 19, Jim taught her how to drive a car. Before that, she'd had no prior interest in obtaining her license, simply because she feared getting behind the wheel with her father. She saw the pressure and rigidity that her older siblings endured while her father taught them. Amy wanted absolutely no part of that! Jim instilled within her the confidence she needed. He was patient and loving. Together for four years, she finally trusted him, but as her trust in him strengthened, bottled emotions again began to emerge: anger and jealousy, low self-esteem and self-worth, obsessions and depression. The reason for these feelings was that she dreamt of her marriage to James for years and had become impatient. He told her that they had to wait until they saved more money.

Shortly after she began her new job, another piece of her puzzling life manifested: Amy's father became ill. She became very upset and frightened that he was about to die. He suffered for weeks with pain in his lower spine. Nerve damage began to affect his posture and ability to walk. The diagnosis was a tumor on his spine, which required surgery to remove. The surgical procedure was successful; however, the mass was malignant. A lymphatic carcinoma, known as Hodgkin's disease, was present in the various lymph nodes throughout his body. He spent weeks in the hospital, undergoing radiation and chemotherapy. The treatments continued for months.

He was transferred to a hospital 90 minutes away from their home, which meant most of the family could only visit on weekends. Amy's father maintained a healthy, positive attitude and vowed to conquer the disease. He reassured his family that he would be 100 % well once again, in no time at all.

Amy feared her father would pass on and blamed herself for his condition. Her constant phobia about his presence—and surely her aversion for him—must have caused his illness. She must have unconsciously wished something wicked would happen to him, which caused Amy a continual flow of self-induced punishment.

In the car with James on a few occasions, she'd light a match and after blowing it out, press it against the skin on her forearm, to intentionally burn herself. She began a short period of self-harm. Sit-ups or crunches she did in the evening, around 100 a day, which led to a muscle tightening pain for days afterward. At certain times when she ate, she had difficulty swallowing and felt like she was choking. It was then that she started to cut back on food intake. Anytime she had a feeling of fullness, she eliminated that particular food from her diet.

As for her mother, she plunged into further denial of the diagnosis, and her depression. The word "cancer" was not spoken in the seventies. Cancer was a curse; it meant death. How would she survive without her husband? How would she provide for her family? How could she run the household alone? She'd have to learn how to drive. How could she possibly make decisions? Who would help her? Mrs. Montgomery compiled one worry after another. Amy heard every one and did not know how to respond to her mother's despair. She was certainly no comfort to Amy. The love and support came from Jim.

After eight weeks, her father was discharged from the hospital. His "pleasing daughter" constructed a "Welcome Home" banner, the first thing he would see upon his arrival through the front door. She wanted a reminder of her in his heart to show him how much she missed him. Amy spent hours with construction paper and colorful markers creating the design. She used masking tape to position the banner above the doorway. "Would it be to his liking, she pondered?" "Would he find a flaw in it?"

Amy's father was surprised when he saw the greeting. He was a bit thinner and ashen-colored, and he walked with a cane, but she was glad he was home—even though atmosphere in their home took on a greater sense of panic.

Her father continued to have weekly chemotherapy treatments. Eric drove him back and forth to the hospital before his own workday began. Amy realized how powerful the medications affected her father's body. After a few short hours, her father became violently ill, with continual vomiting, and then suffered from complete insomnia. She also began to realize the effect these treatments were having on her.

The symptoms of her early adolescence had begun to reappear, the shakiness and trembling, happening most often when she anticipated her father's nausea and retching. One particular day, when he came in the front door, she ran outside and crouched alongside a shrub in the backyard. She was petrified to see or hear him! What was happening to her? She was frightened, and no one was there to help her. She never told anyone how she felt that day. She was embarrassed and ashamed for the way she reacted. After that, the anxiety attacks occurred more frequently. She began to feel as though a demon dwelled inside of her. Years of internalizing verbal and emotional abuse still filled her soul, feelings she had never expressed or released. She was choking on them.

The emotional trauma led to physical trauma: the sight and sound of anyone about to choke or to become ill sent Amy into a panic. What she consumed as nourishment became an issue, even at this very young age in her life. When she experienced the slightest bit of indigestion, upset stomach or a sense of fullness after meals, she omitted these bothersome foods from her diet. It was a slow-moving, gradual process of elimination.

Amy was clueless about what lay ahead of her.

Lake Beverly

At the age of 55, when Joseph, the youngest, was 10 years old, Amy's father retired on disability, the cancer in a state of remission. Free from his daily labor and the resulting stress, his future goals were to become cancer-free and spend all the time he could at the family summer cottage in Ontario, Canada.

For nearly 15 years, the family reserved the cabin each summer, traveling to their haven on Lake Beverly for two weeks in June. On the lake, a sense of peace and tranquility prevailed. The lake was serene, the smell of pine filling the air, and the fish were plentiful. This was a true feeling of family togetherness at this site. The children played outdoors, going on different adventures. They fished, went on boat rides and always took care of the friendly chipmunks with plenty of hard-shell peanuts. Each summer, the family was reunited with their Canadian neighbors, who rented or owned cabins nearby.

Thinking about Canada brought up good feelings for Amy. Her father was a different person there, relaxed, and not angry. Instead of yelling or ignoring her, he taught her things about the outdoors, nature, wildlife and the environment. He had a unique adoration and passion for the place, his escape from the real world.

Amy recalled her excitement as a child, as they arose before dawn to ready themselves for their departure on the six-hour journey. The anticipation was overwhelming, as they packed the station wagon and loaded everyone inside. Each city they passed through was a milestone, with particular landmarks for which the children searched. Closer and closer to the Canadian border, they all tried to be the first to spy the monumental 1,000 Islands Bridge. After passing through the Canadian border, Amy could sense her father's enthusiasm growing, even as she felt their vehicle accelerate, traveling on the familiar dirt roads toward the cottage. She knew every turn, every bump and hill, including the site where the first glimpse of the lake appeared on her right. When the car wound the final turn, she would imagine how she would run down to the dock, the very edge of the dock, to greet Lake Beverly and all of its beauty.

As the migrating geese ventured south for the winter and north in the spring, Amy's father followed the same sequence after his retirement: to the cottage in the spring, and back home in the fall. "God's land," he called it, his savior, his salvation and his cure from the cancer. All throughout the winter months in Pennsylvania, he planned renovations and projects, handcrafting unique pieces for the cottage. All his shortcomings aside, he was a talented, creative man.

Amy's mother continued with her job in the bank. Each summer, when one of the children took a vacation to the lake, she met with her husband. Otherwise, they remained separated for many months out of the year. Mrs. Montgomery managed all the daily responsibilities, decisions, finances and child-care, while her husband was on holiday. Their marital arrangement was difficult for her at times. Amy began to support her mother in every way she could. This lovely young woman, about to begin a life for herself with James, was obligated to step in for her missing father.

Mrs. Montgomery leaned heavily on her daughter, who received nothing but resentment and disappointment from one parent, and then daily doses of chronic complaints and depressive statements from the other. Ailment upon ailment troubled her mother, adding to her distress. Innocent Amy suppressed her responses to her mother's unhappiness, turning them inward. Emotionally, Amy suffered in secret.

As a teenager, Amy had spent most of her time at the lake in solitude. She would arise at dawn and walk onto the dock, squatting down on the very edge of it. She would close her eyes and listen: A slight breeze whisked across the calm water. Birds awoke and began their spectacular cadences, each one uniquely different, harmonizing articulately with one another. Chipmunks and squirrels chimed in, voicing their fancy clicking sounds to summon their American friends for peanuts. Her favorite morning voice was the spine-tingling call of the loon, a beautiful bird, with black-and-white checkerboard feathers and ruby-red eyes. Theirs was a rather silly, piercing cry. A male and female remained together, usually for their lifespan, which was something Amy's father taught her. She would listen to the blue jays, herons, crows and blackbirds, woodpeckers, geese, chickadees, wild canaries and the distant bass croak of the bullfrog. Each morning refreshed her soul with a sense of peace, as all God's delicate creations awoke before her. She welcomed it with all of her heart, this peace for which Amy ached and longed. The breeze would flutter across her face, the distinct aroma of the lake filling her nostrils and the scent of evergreen pine surrounding her.

Engines gliding across the lake, ferrying anglers to their favorite fishing spots, the sound of distant motorboats would soon engulf the quiet. The breeze upon the lake would rise, maple and oak leaves rustling and slight ripples appearing on the lake's surface, making their way to the shoreline with greater force. Small fish surfaced to feed with gentle splashes, and the birds soared gracefully above her. She would breathe deeply, open her eyes and thank God for the beauty on the earth. Then she would stand and stretch, venturing up the stairway and into the cottage.

Her father was always awake inside, nursing his coffee and cigarette, a project already in mind to fill his day. He kept the grounds so beautiful, planted flowers, mowed, weeded and created birdhouses. He had a distinct limp after the surgery, one she could well envision. God, she believed had granted her father another chance at life, a time of transformation, a time of realization. Cancer had threatened him; Canada was his cure.

Amy visited a certain secluded spot each day, for many hours in fact, an area not far from the cottage, on a steep, rock-formed incline. There she read, did puzzles and sunbathed for many an afternoon. It was her place, her peace and her solitude. The most picturesque time of the day was when the sunset colored the sky across the lake, near the old boathouse. The vibrant colors of blazing orange, yellow, shades of pink, blue, lavender and brilliant gold cascaded across the evening sky. Hundreds of photographs had been taken of that view, and each one was different from the other.

The picture of perfection was shattered whenever the neighbors dropped in for a visit. Her father would open the handcrafted cupboard, where the liquor was stored and set ice-filled stemware on the table. The merriment began: whiskey, wine, scotch and rum— on some days, beer or ale. His friends called him the "rich American." He was retired, and yet always served them the best booze.

Hours went by before the company departed, and dinner was often late. Amy's mother sat patiently, interacting with her husband's friends. Amy retreated to her hideaway, safe in seclusion. Drinking meant danger and fear to her, bringing with it her father's badgering, cursing and belittling. When the evening drew to an end, he was intoxicated, usually passed out in his lounge chair. Sometimes, he became stubborn and quarrelsome, disorderly and incorrigible. The worst nights were when he decided to take the boat out for a spin in his drunken condition. Amy loathed him when he drank.

Unfortunately, his drinking wasn't limited to their vacation cabin—or to the evening hours. On one painful Friday, a few hours before her mother came home from work, Amy was in the parlor when her father stumbled in through the front door, drunk. She stood unnoticed in the corner of the room as he passed her and ran into the kitchen to vomit into the sink.

Amy froze, like a statue, torn between running up the stairs to escape that horrible sound of vomiting and staying where she was, so her father wouldn't see her. She could not utter a sound. What would he do if he realized she had seen him? She was so frightened. How could she disappear?

Her father climbed the stairs and fell into his bed. Amy sighed in gratitude: She had survived another episode of terror.

United in Marriage

On April 28, 1979, James and Amy were married. They had been together six years. Amy had always known, with all her heart, that marriage was their destiny. Engaged on Christmas Eve in 1978, they planned their wedding as quickly as possible, holding the ceremony at St John's Nepomocene Church, with a dinner and dance reception at the Stage Coach Inn. They planned a honeymoon trip to San Francisco, Lake Tahoe and Las Vegas.

Surprisingly, and much to their disappointment, James brother and his fiancée decided to plan their wedding one month before their date in April. When Amy thought the center of attention was focused on their announcement, it was quickly taken away. Amy never disclosed to them how she truly felt about their sudden announcement. She and James were very hurt. Amy carried her resentment for many years afterward.

Initially and naturally, Amy wanted a small, quiet, no frill celebration. She reminisced about her brother John and Mary's, quaint and sweet. With both families rather widespread with relatives, Amy consented to a larger affair. Their wedding was a traditionally family-and-friends affair, with 250 invited guests. Ann, Amy's eldest sister, stood as her matron of honor, with James's brother, Brian, as best man. Knowing she had to keep expenses at a minimum, Amy decided to wear her mother's wedding dress, which only needed dry cleaning and a new headdress, adorned with silk flowers. Long-sleeved with a scalloped neckline, the form-fitting gown was made of white printed taffeta with delicate embroidery and beading; the neckline was trimmed with seed pearls. A six-foot train, edged with a wide ruffle, trailed behind her, and 25 buttons adorned her spine. In the gown, Amy felt like the essence of beauty.

That Saturday in late April was picture perfect. The brilliant blue sky and cool spring temperatures brought some relief to Amy's wedding-day jitters, and the day flew by so quickly, seamless and beautiful. Finally united as one, Amy's dreams had come true: they would be together forever, make a new beginning. She loved this man more than she loved herself.

After their honeymoon, they moved into a small, second-story apartment once owned by Amy's family. Mr. Montgomery wallpapered, laid linoleum in the kitchen and set up their appliances. Amy and James scrubbed and scoured the rooms of the quaint, four-room apartment. After a few days, they went back to their local jobs and began this new phase of their lives together.

Throughout her wedding preparations, Amy's pleasing personality prevailed, especially in her father's presence. Although her wedding was supposed to be about James and her, she overextended herself to agree to her father's requests and suggestions about the apartment. Her apprehension of him escalated until it affected her interactions with friends and family. Once again, she internalized her anxieties: Externally, she was the picture of perfection. In time, a creeping depression emerged and began to wreak havoc on the person she loved the most, her husband.

Their first years of marriage were not easy. Isolation and unrealistic demands tested their marriage. Amy needed James unconditionally, and James needed companionship and socialization with friends and family. She was possessive and resentful toward him, becoming infuriated when he attended sports activities and competitive events. Demoralized since early childhood, she had learned to deprive herself of any gratification. When socializing led to a few beers, her anger increased. In her disordered mind, engaging in personal pleasure was unacceptable. She'd ignore James for days, refusing to speak to him. She again began to feel as though she had two personalities, two separate beings dwelling within her that she shared only with James. He had a genuine love for her. For better or worse, he stayed by her side. Day after day, she tested him to be certain that he truly loved her—for no one ever had. She had to make sure that he would never hurt or leave her.

After four years in the apartment, the couple decided it was time to move into a larger home and begin a family. Amy's grandmother's home, a half-double home located on the corner of Chestnut and Maple streets, was available for them to purchase. The house was in dire need of renovation, but Mr. Montgomery happily and eagerly agreed to remodel whatever was within his capability, turning over the rest to his brother and a hired contractor.

Disposition of the house's contents stirred up conflict within the family. Amy's mother had inherited the property from her own mother, while her brother had inherited property in New Jersey. Mrs. Montgomery allowed her brother whatever items he wished from the homestead, a decision that infuriated her husband. Amy remembered her father's slanderous comments and the disgust he displayed toward her uncle when he came to go through his deceased mother's things. One evening, her father got drunk at a local bar, walked home, took the car and drove to the Lake Beverly cottage without saying a word to anyone. Intoxicated and temper-flared, he ran off to his home away from home. Mrs. Montgomery was frantic with worry, but she knew where he had gone to calm himself. Amy could not function until she called him herself, to make sure he had arrived safely. It was just another situation with which Amy's mother should have dealt, but instead left to her daughter.

If her father and mother had ever mended their feelings or spoken words of forgiveness, Amy never knew about it. Her compliant mother agreed to everything "HE" said. When he returned, he began to work on the house immediately, laboring night and day. Jim and Amy helped out when they could, after their workday; usually until 9:00 or 10:00 P.M. Mr. Montgomery's goal was to have the home ready for them in six months, in the spring. Of course, for him the spring meant heading north. They had to be settled in before he left for the cottage.

Was his long labor an escape from his wife, or was it a labor of love for Amy? Was he truly there to help his daughter by refurbishing her home? Was his hard work the affection for which Amy had longed? Amy never knew the answers to any of these questions. Her feelings were tangled, distorted and confused. Mostly, she felt sad and uncertain that her parents really did not love one another, and she felt the fear of her father every single day.

They took photographs before, during and after the renovation was complete, going room by room. Mr. Montgomery's brother, a skilled master craftsman and a gifted artist, hand-constructed new kitchen cabinets. A perfectionist with amazing talent, Amy's uncle also built spectacular pieces of furniture, sailing ships, intricate dollhouses and children's toys. The cabinets were solid wood, made of oak. They were flawless.

Throughout the renovation, many decisions had to be made. Ceiling tile, paneling, paint color, bathroom and lighting fixtures, countertops and tile. Everything had to be chosen, right down to the carpeting. The decision-making overwhelmed Amy. She relied on her father's input, naturally, in her mind; he'd make the proper choices. How could she possibly approach him if she had a different perspective on things? His way was always the right way.

Mr. Montgomery painted and paneled the walls and inserted ceiling tiles. He stumbled upon an antique-wood corner hutch that had five coats of white paint on it and meticulously stripped the hutch down to its natural wood grain, refinishing the piece for their kitchen. Smaller jobs included rewiring, adding light fixtures, laying linoleum, purchasing appliances and installing wall-to-wall carpet. As spring drew nearer, Amy sensed her father's anxiety and anticipation of the finished project.

May 3, 1983, was moving day. Mr. Montgomery went north on May 5. Amy drove to her homestead early that morning to bid farewell to her father. She hugged him and told him, "I love you, Dad." He said, "I love you, too. See you in the summer." It was the first time Amy could remember him ever saying he loved her.

Throughout the entire project, Mrs. Montgomery remained distant, rarely coming to witness any part of the transformation. Amy presumed the differences between her mother and her uncle, as well as her mother's degenerative health conditions, asthma foremost, kept her away; her uncle was at the house most of the time, and the air-quality conditions were poor at various times. However, deep inside, Amy sensed her mother was upset with the fact that her childhood home had been taken away from her and been drastically changed. It was no longer graying, uninviting or depressing, but alive, restored and brand-new, a happy dwelling place for her daughter and son-in-law. Amy felt guilty for taking away her mother's childhood memories. No longer were the pieces of furniture in their proper places, a tiny pantry no longer offset the kitchen, and the old swing on the back porch was gone. Amy had destroyed something in her mother, and she visited very seldom.

Slowly, piece-by-piece, her mother was breaking Amy down. Her mother's low self-confidence and self-worth, her progressive ailments and deteriorating health, all made her feel dependent, despondent and disheartened. The many years of her mother's behavior gradually took Amy downward, too. Amy tried to remain cheerful about her new surroundings, but it was becoming increasingly difficult.

Within a year after the move, they purchased a cocker-spaniel puppy from a private breeder. Amy loved the Disney movie *Lady and the Tramp* as a child, and the spaniel had always been her favorite. They named their dog "Dusty," and loved him a great deal. Puppies are always adorable, but Dusty was invigorating. He was more than active—more like hyperactive. He barked, jumped, spun in circles, chewed the rugs and furniture, and, when overexcited, he'd urinate all over the house. He also did not travel well. Amy blamed herself for his behavior. She felt she was a poor trainer and the dog's disposition was a sort of punishment for her. She deserved the strain this puppy was causing. Nevertheless, he was adorable, he was Amy's, and she loved him.

In the spring of 1984, for their fifth anniversary, Jim and Amy decided to help her father open the cottage. In late April, they took

Dusty and followed behind him for the six-hour journey. Something happened that weekend that forever affected Amy's psyche. Throughout their stay for those three days, a continual flow of Canadian geese returned from their southern migration. Hundreds upon hundreds, flock after flock, flew overhead in their methodical v-shaped pattern. James, Amy and her father listened to the familiar honking sounds, so prominent and perseverant in the sky. They were joyous cries, as the geese returned to their chosen homeland, the lakes of Canada.

Amy remembered how she and her father stood on the dock and gazed above, pointing and listening to the geese. A feeling overwhelmed her that day, an indescribable feeling! The sight and sound of the geese returning home meant warmer days ahead, that spring had arrived. A marvelous feeling swept over her, a sigh of relief from the winter months. Was it because in the spring, her father took off with the geese for the cottage, returning home in the fall, when the geese flew south? Had she missed him? Was she happy that he had gone? Later in her lifetime, after her father had passed on, her response to the sound of migrating geese was apprehension and panic. She gasped, cringed and covered her ears, trying to get away from the raucous noise.

As she grew older, obsessive-compulsive behaviors more frequently overwhelmed her. In the spring and fall, she hesitated before going outdoors, afraid that she'd hear honking geese. She became so keen to the sound that she began to hear them indoors. Was she searching for her father, or did he continuously haunt her? Was it the realization that he'd never be home again? It was a phobia, one of many that controlled her daily living.

After many more years, the severity of her reactions diminished. As far as her children knew, she loved geese. Eventually, the association became positive, as memories of the lake became stronger than memories of her troubled childhood. However, Amy always retained mixed emotions, fear and love and devotion, whenever she saw or heard migrating geese. She yearned for the attachment and affection her father expressed to her in his last few years. After he was gone, she missed him. That spring get-away created an indelible memory. After he retired, she finally got the chance to know him. She wished they'd had more time.

Firstborn Son

A joyful event occurred on June 17, 1985, at 6:39 P.M.- Jim and Amy's first child was born, named Jim respectfully after his father. Thankfully, Amy's labor lasted less than three hours, after which her father-in-law had this to say: "No one can properly prepare an individual for parenthood! It doesn't come equipped with a manual, and it's the toughest job in the world."

Amy expected parenthood to be a "piece of cake." She thought everything came naturally, with ease. What could be hard about taking care of a child? Wasn't it just a matter of bottle- feeding, changing diapers, and the baby slept during the first few weeks? She wasn't worried; she had James to help her. She was oblivious to the fact that she might feel discomfort for a few weeks after giving birth, or that infant's cry until their needs are met, and sometimes the parents may not know what their child may need at a given time. This was without mentioning about how her emotions may be in a bit of a state as well. She soon came to the realization after giving birth and coming home that becoming a parent is a major change in your life.

When James Jr. was born, Dusty was two years old. Amy and James wondered how their little dog would react to their infant's homecoming. Worried about jealousy and an animal's protective instincts, Amy held and rocked a baby doll for weeks prior to the delivery, hoping Dusty would become accustomed to the small bundle in her arms. She brought out infant layettes, baby powders and lotions. A friend of hers suggested a "mock" preparation for her pet. The transition went well and they began to settle in.

The abrupt change from full-time employment outside the home to full-time mother inside the home had a turbulent effect on Amy. She had hemorrhaged substantially after the birth and was rather weak when she returned home. She was light-headed and experienced extreme fatigue when she did something as simple as climbing her stairs. They were exhausted new parents, indeed, and Amy soon felt overwhelmed by the many changes that were happening.

Postpartum depression was a given. After James Jr. was born, she became obsessed about her birthing process. Every Monday, at exactly 6:39 P.M., she psychologically replayed the experience—each Monday, for months. Afraid to tell anyone about her feelings, she'd tell herself that they now had a son, and he was solely their responsibility. She somehow had to accept things the way they were; it was her lot as a mother to feel tired and weighed down all the time.

As the weeks and months passed, Jim's domineering mother interfered with Amy's life every day, giving her childrearing "advice," making demands and imposing on Amy's already-overloaded schedule. Her mother-in-law meant well, but she upset Amy terribly. She received daily doses of instructions: feed the baby cereal at this time of day, always have socks on his feet and a hat on his head, and do not take that child out of the house until his Baptism! No pacifiers, just formula with Karo syrup to keep his bowels moving regularly, and lay him on his belly to sleep. Mrs. Bailey absolutely despised the fact that Amy nursed her son. She was controlling and overbearing, to say the least, and Amy felt as though everything she was doing was wrong. "God," Amy thought, "Whose child is this, hers or mine?" Amy soon began to resent her mother- in- laws comments and her mother- in- law as well! She was shocked at how she had changed her attitude after Jim was born! As usual, she internalized her unhappiness, feeling so full of negative emotions that she felt as though her emotions would overflow at any time.

In July, Amy's father surprised her: He came home from Lake Beverly to see his new grandson and partake in the Baptismal ceremony and celebration. Amy was elated! She meant something to him! He had come home for her and her family. Remembering the very moment that he walked through her back door to greet her, she discovered that her trust in him was maturing, something she had thought would never happen.

Autumn approached. Cooler temperatures brought Daylight Savings Time and longer, darker evenings. Jim Jr. came down with his first illness, bronchitis. Amy was already easily agitated, exhausted and overwhelmed with the responsibilities of parenthood, and now her level of anxiety became out of control. James Jr.'s fever, congestion and cough made Amy tremble with worry. With every decision she made, every situation with which she was confronted, her anxiety intensified. She wanted her life calm and without worry; she wanted perfection. She felt immature, unaware of how to deal with her emotions.

Slowly, she succumbed to depression, pessimism, self-hatred and pain. In the New Year, she searched for a crutch to ease her distress, narrowing it down to two alternatives: alcohol or cigarettes. She chose to smoke again. In their high school days, Jim and Amy had smoked a little. He was the first to quit; Amy had a very troublesome time with it, suffering from mood swings, irritability and crying spells as the nicotine left her body. Eventually, she kicked the habit, but in the process, she hit rock bottom. Now, unable to ask for help, she had to take control of her life by punishing herself, so she began smoking again. Her inner self was destroyed, so she began a gradual process of killing her outer, physical being.

Driven to torture herself, she began the process of total self-destruction, depriving herself of anything that gave her joy. In March of that year, Amy placed an ad in her local newspaper, reading "Free to a good home, two-year-old male cocker spaniel." Within two days, a gentleman telephoned and expressed his interest in Dusty. She never questioned the man about his background or whether or not he had children. He came to her house, said he would be happy to take Dusty home with him and handed her his telephone number. Dusty jumped into his pick-up truck, and they drove away. Amy's heart was shattered. For weeks she imagined that she heard his familiar bark. She was grief-stricken, guilt-ridden and could not speak of what she had done; she told James that she could no longer deal with Dusty's temperament. Her husband did not stop her from giving him away, which led Amy to believe that they would be happier without him.

Summer approached, and Jim had his first birthday. She and James threw him a party in the backyard, inviting family and friends. They had a cookout on the grill, a homemade cake and lots of presents. Amy remembered a special photograph taken with her parents and in-laws seated in lawn chairs, on that perfectly sunlit day. Her father, who had already made his spring migration to the cottage, came home briefly for a physical exam. He appeared pale, withdrawn and ill at ease. Only in later years did Amy realize what his appearance signified.

At the time of James Jr.'s first birthday, Mr. Montgomery was almost 10 years in remission from Hodgkin's disease, but his health condition began to deteriorate. He weakened and had difficulty breathing. Blood transfusions became necessary, as his bone marrow no longer produced an adequate blood supply for his body to function normally. In his immortal mind, the transfusions increased his energy level. Rejuvenated, he drove to the lake, where he experienced peace and healing from God. Within one week, Eric brought him back home. The transfusions became weekly; his condition worsened. He continued to lead his family to believe in his full recovery.

The Christmas of 1986, Amy's entire family came home. Amy stitched a crewel picture for her father's gift: he adored Japanese décor, so she stitched an image of a bud-sprouting Japanese bonsai tree. Beneath, intermixed around the tree, were long threads of multi-hued blades of grass. She presented it to him on Christmas Day, unframed. He admired the creation and the intricate stitching. Amy was pleased that he loved it.

The first of the year brought Amy's mother's birthday, the second, her father's. Amy had the picture framed for the occasion, and she, James and James Jr. visited with them on that cold, wintry evening.

Mr. Montgomery sat in his favorite recliner, admired the framed picture and dozed in and out of sleep. A portable oxygen unit rested by his side; he was very frail. Two days after Amy's birthday, on January 14, he was admitted to the hospital. The family was called to his bedside late that afternoon, but by the time James and Amy arrived, her father had passed away. As they stood by his side, Amy repeated, "I love you, Dad. I love you, Dad." James gently guided her out of the hospital room to gather with the rest of her family in the lobby.

They all were numb, empty and expressionless; darkness and disbelief had overcome them. Their father had not kept his promise—he was not immortal. The family wandered through the days that followed, the funeral services and burial. The day they laid him to rest was bone-chilling and bitter cold. Two of Mr. Montgomery.'s Canadian friends—from Lake Beverly, her father's home away from home, his utopia, and his haven—traveled to Pennsylvania to pay their final respects. Little James was only 19 months old when his grandfather died. He may not retain a vivid memory of his grandfather, but he would have many good memories from the summers spent at the lake thereafter. Mr. Montgomery had always stated that the cottage, his legacy to them, would be there for his entire family to enjoy.

A black cloud enshrouded Amy from that day on. She lost any sense of "self" or "herself," giving most of her time and energy to Jim Jr. After her father died, her mother needed her desperately, and time for Amy's own husband dwindled tremendously. She had no time, energy, hope or inclination to take care of herself. Her mind and body were slowly taken over by a demon, some other person inside of her, who began to control her thoughts and actions. Her appetite diminished. Little by little, she continued to eliminate more and more foods from her diet. With each new day, it became increasingly hard for her to make a decision. She overreacted to basic situations and small complications or disappointments.

Once again, Amy had support from her husband, but not one ounce from her own mother. Thankfully, Mrs. Montgomery continued to work at the bank, which kept her mind occupied from nine to five. She was among her friends and co-workers, as well as the general public. Yet Amy sensed how sad her mother had become and understood her grief. Her other brothers and sisters helped out when they could, but because Amy was at home with little James, she was the one child available to her whenever she needed help, the only child who would meet her mother's needs. Amy became the chauffer, driving her mother to the grocery store, to doctor appointments and to the hairdresser. Amy told herself that she didn't mind; after all, her mother had never learned how to drive.

Amy gave every inch of herself, listening to her mother's unhappiness and complete dejection, complaints about everything and everyone. Turning her own unhappiness inward, Amy no longer had the words to comfort her mother or try to pick her back up. Amy was slowly submitting to depression, just like her mother; she knew was destined to become just like her, with her complaints, her compliancy and her bottomless despair.

After living a life colored by depression, Mrs. Montgomery had difficulty expressing love to her children. A simple hug always felt cold and meaningless to Amy, as though there was a wall or a barrier between them. Amy could count on one hand the number of times her mother had babysat for James Jr. Whenever Amy asked, she would say she was afraid of suffering an asthmatic attack or simply that she did not feel well. To Amy, it felt as though her mother disliked her own grandchildren. All she talked about were her problems, her deteriorating health, her doctor's visits and prescriptions.

Amy kept to herself. She and little James were "homers," concealed in the house for most of his toddler years. He loved to watch *Sesame Street* and occupied his time playing with cars, trucks and action figures. They read books, built with Lego's and played outside in the yard. Because their home was within one block of the fire station, Jim Jr. could peer out the kitchen window to see if the firehouse doors were open. "Doors are open, Mom!" he'd shout, and off they'd go, hand in hand, to visit the vehicles inside. They were very content with one another at home.

James was born with a congenital abdominal hernia, medically defined as an internal muscle protrusion through a weakened area of the abdomen. He had a noticeable lump, and his pediatrician examined him every six months for any changes. At two years of age, it was surgically repaired. Preparation for the surgery involved urine samples, blood work and frequent doctor visits, but the surgery was performed as an outpatient procedure. James was released the same day and recovered remarkably well, as their physician had said he would.

The pre-operative and post-operative procedures debilitated her. Amy could have asked for support throughout this difficult time, however she made the decision to do it alone. She felt it was solely her responsibility. Her anxiety became intense and her shakiness returned. It was unbearable for her to see her son poked, prodded, and restrained to get through the appointments. On the eve before and the morning of the surgery, Jim could not have any food or liquids. It was difficult to tell him he could have nothing until the days end. Her husband was by her side when they entered the hospital that morning. Together they walked him to the operating room, and released him to the physician and anesthesiologist. She remembered how he cried when they left him. Relieved when the surgery was over, they rejoined Jim in the recovery room and later to his hospital room. Young Jim was groggy and sick to his stomach for most of the day. By 4:00 P.M., they arrived back home. They were emotionally exhausted. Amy had hardly eaten a bite all day long.

Amy needed professional help and antidepressants, but she didn't realize there was anything that could help her. Her cigarette smoking increased, her phobias intensified, and her self-destruction lingered. Feeling comfortable with her isolation, Amy withdrew even further. Jim Sr. arrived home after work each day and found her and Jim Jr. indoors, the windows closed. She became obsessed with meticulous needlework. Cross-stitch embroidery was her passion, one design after another. She sat at a barstool in her kitchen, hour after hour, as she smoked and stitched. Many days, she failed to prepare meals for her husband. She had slipped into a world of her own, dysfunctional and deranged.

Amy continued the dangerous cycle, eliminating foods from her diet, foods she claimed upset her stomach. She was subconsciously replacing her uncontrollable emotions, her anxiety, fear and depression, with a masterful control over food. With each deletion, she felt triumphant, as though she had crushed a particular feeling. Deleted pasta meant erasure of the horrifying experience in fourth grade, when she was sick, while her father was at home and her mother was bowling. Pizza, eggs, soup, hamburgers, fish and pastries crushed the sadness, tension, shame and verbal abuse that characterized her childhood.

Each food that fell from her diet was a huge victory for her. She had control! She was in control! When she restricted food, she had accomplished something. She was someone, and she was on top of the world! Although she had no control over anything else in her life, she had control over food. What satisfaction she felt!

A time came when she felt sick as she watched other people eat. *How could they eat that? How can they eat that amount of food?* As the weeks and months passed by, tension arose between her and James. Although neither of them noticed her change on any particular day, she slipped into a deeply depressive state, a condition that did not occur overnight. It was a long process, a pattern that unfolded over a period of years.

One and a half years after Mr. Montgomery died, in July of 1988, her father-in-law passed away, little James's "Pap," at the age of 72. Cancer took his life, just as it had taken Amy's father. Strangely, Jim's family handled Mr. Bailey's demise much differently than Amy's family had dealt with her father's passing. Surely, they grieved! But the family was not devastated, instead becoming even closer to one another. Amy's mother-in-law, Nanny, as she was called, had such religious faith and strength—she always seemed to know what had to be done. Everyone helped her, and she was always there for her family.

Amy had barely grieved for her own father, and now her father-in-law was being laid to rest. She was nauseated and felt faint, never realizing how low her blood pressure was. She continued to smoke a pack—sometimes more—a day. At five in the morning, she arose, consuming coffee and cigarettes to the point of daily cramping and diarrhea. For three years, perhaps more, she kept up that ritual. Her reward was the satisfaction she felt for having a completely flat stomach—after emptying her body with her "poor-man's laxative," caffeine and nicotine.

Continued food restriction helped her through the first holidays and special occasions without two parents. She saw the pain in both mothers' eyes. Nanny was open, talking and crying with her family. Her mother was the opposite, refusing to shed a tear. Amy's family was not allowed to feel emotions.

After his first surgery, health problems continued to plague young Jim. Another lower abdominal hernia protruded, on the opposite side, which required another surgical repair. A few months later, Jim and Amy noticed that their son's left eye started to float inward, toward his nose. A pediatric ophthalmologist in Philadelphia diagnosed James Jr. as being extremely far-sighted. His left eye attempted to focus simultaneously with the right, hence the inward turning. The condition was corrected with eyeglasses with powerful lenses; behind them, his tiny, three-year-old eyes seemed unnaturally magnified.

Amy could not understand why little James had gone through so many complications in his first few years. She continued to ask herself why... Why was this happening to their son? What had he done? Eventually, the question became, "What had Amy done?" She must be punished, for she had done everything wrong. She no longer considered herself fit to be his mother. She had not nurtured, guided, or kept him from harm. No longer was she a wife to her husband, either. She was angry and distant and had formed a protective barrier between them, so that she wouldn't be able to hurt him. She lived in her own isolated world, an invisible, ghostlike non-person, out of necessity hidden from the outside world. The demon was taking control over her body and soul.

Amy continued to feel triumphant whenever she weighed herself in the morning and read the same result each evening, before she retired. Her goal each day was to see how long she could go without eating—2:00 P.M., 3:00 P.M., and 4:00 P.M. Smoking curbed her appetite or gave her such terrible cramping and discomfort that she was unable to eat. The numbers on the scale continued to dip lower. When James turned four, Amy weighed 95 lbs., several pounds lighter than she'd been since junior high school.

Amy had not realized or accepted the fact that her son was very tuned in to her feelings, temperament and state of mind. Amy's problems were beginning to affect her son. He was adorable, but shy and easily frustrated, clinging to his mother. Even the smallest changes in his routine caused crying spells. His vision accounted for his disposition to a certain degree—he became cranky and upset when he couldn't see correctly—but Amy attributed the remainder of his personality on her own behavior, just another bit of proof that she was an inadequate mother.

At age five, and continuing for years after, little James underwent phases of "night fright." Usually, within an hour after he fell asleep, he awoke and cried for his mother, unaware of his surroundings and very fearful. He appeared to be in a state of delirium, pacing and complaining of disoriented vision. First, he moaned and shouted out, "Mom, Mom," "Where's my Mom?" He'd say, "I want my Mom."

"I'm right here Jim," Amy said. She'd take his hands and look into his eyes. "I am right here." She embraced him and tried to awaken him. He'd wander around his room. Amy always called for James to help calm him. After a few minutes, Jim and Amy succeeded in awaking him fully and helped him relax and get back to sleep. Sometimes, the episode recurred within another hour.

Were these problems caused by television or particular foods eaten late? Or was it his mother?

Shutdown and Hospitalization

In September of 1990, James Jr. entered kindergarten. From pre-school to public school, the transition was seamless for little James. For his mother, it was her final shutdown.

On his first day of school, her son stood at the front door, dressed in his new outfit and sneakers, carrying his red Garfield lunchbox, a wide grin from ear to ear. Amy snapped a few photographs, and off they went. When she returned home, she curled up on her living-room couch. Curtains drawn tightly against the daylight, she began to cry. Her father was gone, her mother despondent, her husband worked full-time and she had sent her son off to school. All alone, almost invisible, she was knocked down so low that she was unable to get up. It—whatever "it" was—had completely destroyed her.

In total desperation, Amy finally admitted that something was terribly wrong with her. She asked herself one day in mid-September, "Why am I so afraid of food?" "Why am I so afraid to eat?" "I am counting calories, I am portioning, I am weighing myself a few times a day, I am drinking more fluids, and I am using particular silverware and glassware. I like to be alone, be isolated from people. "I need to eat, to live!" she scolded herself. "Am I going crazy?" "Somebody help me!"

She cried daily, looking back at the past instead of planning ahead and moving forward. She wanted to go back to when her father was alive. She needed to talk to him, to tell him how sorry she was for never getting to know him. There was so much left unsettled, so much unsaid. She'd never had the chance to say goodbye.

She spoke to her husband. Jim, as always, was very understanding and patient with her. They made an appointment with her family physician, to whom Amy confessed her fear and anxiety attacks, crying spells and trembling episodes. Most importantly, she explained how food consumption had become a major issue.

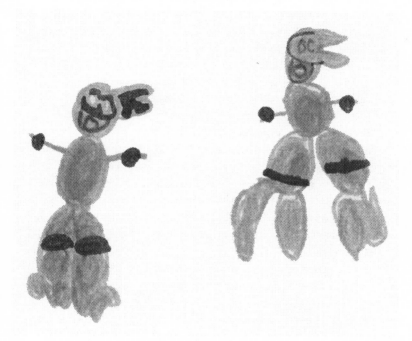

Dr. Davis listened intently to Amy and asked her to keep a log of the foods she had eaten each day. She gave Amy a referral to a female psychologist at Geisinger Medical Center, a hospital forty minutes from Amy's home.

After she made the appointment with the psychologist, Amy needed to tell her family about her situation. Naturally, she was embarrassed and ashamed, but she managed to tell them, stumbling over the words until they were all out. Next, she found more courage and drove to the hospital for her scheduled appointment. As she drove, the tension became unbearable; she was trembling violently by the

time she parked her car. As she stepped onto the elevator to the third-floor office, her heart throbbed. She felt weak and about to faint.
What was the matter with her?

During her first visit to Geisinger, Dr. Lora made her feel somewhat comfortable. Amy tried to explain everything that had happened to her, emotionally and physically, as best she could. They talked for the allotted hour, while Dr. Lora documented their discussion. She wanted to see Amy on a weekly basis, for one hour each visit. The fee was $125 per visit. *What an expense!* Amy thought. How could she and Jim afford that price every week?

Jim said to Amy, "We will handle these fees."

"The treatment is necessary for you."

And "I want my wife back again."

The following week, Amy began to understand. As she drove to her appointment, she felt less frantic. Dr. Lora began with an explanation of her diagnosis. "Amy," she said, "You are experiencing classic symptoms of an eating disorder called anorexia nervosa."

Amy could not believe what she was hearing! "Anorexia?" she said, "Anorexia is something that happens to teenaged girls! I am not a teenager!"

Amy was outraged. She felt discouraged and depressed. Dr. Lora suggested a very helpful drug, the antidepressant Prozac. If Amy began taking it now, the drug would become effective in approximately four weeks. Dr. Lora also suggested Amy undergo cognitive and behavioral modification therapy, treatment that would bring out the emotional trauma Amy had experienced and repressed. Dr. Lora said that Amy needed to set goals, to try to arrange the scrambled pieces of the intricate jigsaw puzzle that was her life. Amy departed Dr. Lora's office that day feeling more scrambled than ever.

The next step was to relay all of this information to her husband and family. Was this diagnosis really accurate? She recalled in high school how she had idolized the supermodels in fashion magazines. Poised and lean, how they flowed as they walked! Hadn't every young girl in America dreamed of having such beauty and slenderness?

Why was it wrong for her to want the same?

Amy had never known how to dress or dance, let alone put on makeup. She assumed everyone would ridicule her, especially if she asked such foolish questions. How had all the other girls figured it out? Had their mothers helped them? She had always made certain that her stomach was board-flat. Gymnastics were her passion, as was yoga; she envisioned herself cross-legged, spine erect and in perfect posture. Daily sit-ups and 10 to 15 minutes of hoola hoop activity punctuated her days back then, as she well recalled. She had done whatever she needed to keep her body in shape.

Early in her marriage when she first gave up cigarettes, she'd walk for miles to release the cravings and keep her weight intact. Later, in the new house, an exercise bicycle from a yard sale helped her keep her body lean. At that time, she was 5'6" tall and weighed 112 lbs. She had always been a thin young woman—had this disorder been a part of her life since she was a teenager? The time had come to join the puzzle pieces together.

After Amy's second appointment with Dr. Lora, she approached or telephoned each family member individually, looking for his or her support. She did not want them to think she was crazy. *For God's sake,* she thought, *she was 32 years old, had a five-year-old son and was afraid to eat! How pathetic!* Her brothers and sisters were somewhat shocked, but wanted to be supportive. Her mother, on the other hand, had only blamed herself, which was of no help to Amy.

From her therapy, she learned that the worst question to ask an anorexic was, "What did you have to eat today?" For Amy, that query brought feelings of humiliation and anger. Whenever approached by those words, she'd shut down, cry and recoil. On the other hand, the most helpful of questions were, "How are things going today?" or "How are you feeling today, Amy?" These queries showed genuine concern. Her mother only asked the first question, while her husband and siblings understood they needed to ask the others, to approach Amy on terms she could understand.

Each weekly appointment with Dr. Lora began on the scale. Amy stepped onto it, staring straight ahead, fearing the scale when in the presence of others. Was the number up or down from last week? Dr. Lora understood Amy's situation and watched her very closely. "If the scale dipped to 90 pounds," she told Amy, "You will have to be hospitalized." Amy was at 94 and somehow knew what was about to happen.

Amy did not focus on caloric contents of food. Her body automatically knew what she was ingesting. Her therapist explained that she should compile a list of "safe" foods and beverages, items Amy could ingest without feeling panicky. Whenever she needed sustenance, she should eat her safe foods: toasted bread, baked potatoes, apples, celery, carrots, lettuce, tomatoes, dry cereals and crackers. Ironically, she drank whole milk and regular iced tea, coffee and soda—colorless lemon-lime soda represented untainted purity. She functioned on roughly 700 calories a day.

Amy usually ate alone, or in the presence of her son. She ate very little, every few hours, to maintain a consistent level of energy throughout the day. Timing meant everything. Certain foods were consumed at precisely the same hour each day. If her schedule or rituals were disrupted or overextended, she became extremely irritable and agitated. Amy thought she had control over the eating disorder. What she learned was that it had control over her. She was starving—hungering for what she had been missing in her life.

Every waking moment, even when she awoke during the night, her thoughts were on food: what to eat, when to eat and where to eat. Thought processes focused on food, distorting everything to relate to food. Her eating disorder, her mad obsession with food, totally dictated every aspect of simple daily living with her husband and son. She was trapped inside her body and her mind, completely controlled by anorexia nervosa. *Please,* she cried to herself, *someone let me out!*

During the days prior to a family event, she became more nervous. How could she hide? Everyone would see what she ate. She made excuses, shied away from company, helped the children, washed dishes, any activity to divert herself from the dinner table. As she came to learn from her therapist, she feared the social situation, not the food.

Each week passed, with one therapy session. The numerical reading on the scale slowly dropped. Dr. Lora instructed Amy to write down ten goals for herself, which they would work together to accomplish. In another session, Dr. Lora wanted Amy to try to eat a different food or bring back into her diet a particular food each day. After every appointment, Amy was exhausted and more confused. She could not even think of 10 goals for herself. She felt worthless and unable to achieve anything. Try a new food daily? Amy could not even try a new food weekly!

After one particular Sunday-evening family visit at her mother's house, Amy came home greatly disturbed. Unable to remember the cause of her distress, she thought about consuming her entire container of antidepressants. At her next appointment, she admitted the episode to Dr. Lora and explained how she had felt. Dr. Lora was concerned and instructed Amy to have James distribute her medication. She telephoned James immediately at work.. She feared that Amy was unable to fight the anorexia for much longer.

September, October and November came and went. She made only minimal improvement in her treatment. Dr. Lora's next recommendation was that her husband should come with Amy to her next session. Jim did, of course. That was the day the scale read 90 pounds.

As she stood on the scale, Amy could not make eye contact with the doctor or her husband. She held her head up as she sat down at the table, her arms propped on the table the entire hour. She felt extremely unstable, knowing what was to come next. Dr. Lora needed Jim's consent for Amy's admission to an eating-disorder center in Philadelphia. Dr. Lora advised him to have emergency telephone numbers handy and to notify their local hospital of Amy's degenerative condition. She was no longer capable of caring for herself or for her son. Jim could have legally taken James Jr. away from her. How frightening a thought! Jim swore his everlasting love for her, over and over again, telling her not to worry. He would never take away their son.

Dr. Lora assured them that the program in Philadelphia was excellent. The facility was associated with the Graduate Hospital and was actually located on the 20th floor of the Windsor Hotel, on 17th and Ben Franklin Parkway. The entire floor had been remodeled to accommodate women suffering from eating disorders. A trained, specialized staff was on board: physicians, psychologists, psychiatrists, nutritionists, chefs and social workers. A small community, the residents of the 20th-floor unit were contained and controlled, living by rules and regulations, participating in daily group therapies and individual counseling, having their vital signs monitored and taking distributed medications. The hospitalization was a minimum of 30 days.

They departed Dr. Lora's office in silence, shocked and worried about the upcoming course of treatment. Over that weekend, they prepared; the trip to Philadelphia came on Monday, the week of Thanksgiving. Later, Amy could only vaguely remember what she packed or how she informed her family. She was so ashamed of herself. The most difficult time came when they told their son. They explained that his mother needed to be in a hospital for a little while, to get help so she could feel better. James and Jr. moved in with Nanny. She and Helen, a dear family friend, cared for little Jim. Amy also had a close friend who would transport Jim Jr. back and forth to school. A supportive network of family and friends were with her.

Jim's brother-in-law, Eric, drove them all to Philadelphia on Monday morning. All three were uneasy. When they arrived, they completed the paperwork and signed for admission to the unit. Booklets and pamphlets explained the program, the rules and regulations, daily procedures, restrictions and goals for the residents. Amy's room was the last one on the left, at the end of the hallway. She met her roommate, Donna, who was bulimic.

Jim and Eric waited in the lounge area as the staff members took Amy around the unit. It was one o'clock, and lunch had been served.

The three rejoined in the dining area to have something to eat. The lengthy dining-room table, with ample seating for twenty people was made of wood and the chairs had a dark, walnut finish. Windows lined the far wall of the room, with rooftops in view, where a vast section of the city could be seen from the 20th floor.

Amy sat in the first chair, her back to the windows. Jim was at the head, with Eric across the table from her. A full plate was placed in front of her, but she ate only a few carrot sticks. Later, she could remember nothing else on the dish. She realized the time was drawing near for Jim and Eric to leave her. She walked with them to the elevator, gave Eric a hug and clung to James.

"Please, please don't leave me," she pleaded and began to cry.

The elevator door opened and they stepped inside.

"I love you," Jim said.

The doors closed, and they were gone.

Amy walked to her room, alone and scared. She lay down across the bed and sobbed.

The Graduate Hospital

Within a few minutes, a staff nurse came into Amy's room. Along with her followed Dr. Perry, the Clinical Associate Professor of Psychiatry and the program director of the Eating Disorder Unit. He politely introduced himself to Amy, holding her personal profile and medical-statistics chart. After performing a physical examination, taking her vital signs, blood pressure and pulse, he asked her many questions and developed a specific treatment plan to meet her needs. Dr. Perry assigned a woman named Joann to Amy's case, a nurse who would relay all medical information back to Dr. Perry. They told her to relax and unpack her belongings. Joann then introduced her to the other residents in the unit.

They walked to the lounge, where smoking was allowed. The room was relatively small, just enough of an area to hold a television and a sofa, with ample chairs to seat all the patients comfortably. In the lounge area, residents gathered after each meal, for exactly 45 minutes. Staff counselors assigned to the women were present during their mealtimes, as well, assisting the residents through their "post meal" transition period, a difficult time for people who suffered from eating disorders.

Unaware of the degree of medical danger she was in, Amy began days of extensive psychological therapy, receiving unconditional support. A team of doctors worked closely with the medical staff to help her physically and emotionally. Each day held a full schedule, which kept the women from isolation. Amy attended nutritional counseling every day and individual and family therapies two to three times per week, as well as group, movement, recreational and

72

art therapies throughout the week. Amy needed to be taken care of, to learn how to communicate and socialize with other individuals, and most important, to transform and reconstruct the "inner demon" that had taken control of her mind and body. She and Joann communicated comfortably, and Amy began to form a small sense of trust with her counselor.

The facility's treatment plan was based on three levels: All residents entered at Level I. A registered dietician chose their meals. Amy felt violated when she discovered that each time she needed to use the restroom, it had to be unlocked and monitored by a staff member. The "open door" privilege was awarded when a resident entered Level II. Amy later understood the reason for that rule, which pertained to the women that binged, purged or were dependent upon laxatives. In Level I, Amy was not allowed to leave the unit without supervision, but visitors and telephone calls were welcomed. She received constant staff support and reinforcement as they began to modify her dysfunctional eating patterns and ritualistic habits.

Within one week, most residents advanced to Level II, when they could plan their own meals from the dietician's weekly menu. Her bathroom would be unlocked, and she could obtain a pass to leave the unit with her family, staff members or a resident who had obtained Level-III privileges. As resident's moved closer to their discharge dates, they moved to Level III, which granted an offsite pass and meals outside the facility.

As residents reached a new level, they gained additional responsibilities, enabling them to gain confidence and begin preparation for the transition from their contained, supportive community environment to their familiar home settings. When Amy was discharged from the unit, Joann explained, therapy with Dr. Lora would continue, with the possibility of group therapy, if it were available. Joann reiterated the importance of having strong family support as Amy progressed through the stages of recovery. The first few days were the most difficult, Joann explained. She told Amy that changes and adaptation took time, but she would be Amy's support system for 30 days.

Amy's roommate, Donna, returned from her afternoon pass with her family. Arriving a few days before Amy, Donna had already been hospitalized at two different facilities. Only 19 years old, Donna suffered from anorexia and bulimia. She was tall and athletic and loved to run, but as she uncovered in her therapy, she had been sexually abused as a child. Her disorder sheltered her from the horror of those memories.

Although she tried to exude an aura of confidence and bravado, Amy's true colors soon showed through. After she became acquainted with her new surroundings, she began to panic. It was just about time for her first meal with her fellow residents in the dining hall. She felt such terror as she anticipated what was waiting for her in that room!

Shortly before 5:30 P.M., Joann rejoined Amy and took her to the dining room. Amy was petrified! As Joann walked with Amy, she disclosed what her meals would consist of for the first week of Amy's hospitalization. Each individual had her own eating plan, or EP number. The higher the number, the more calories they consumed; Amy began at EP 5, with the knowledge that her EP number would increase as she began to consume more calories. Meeting this goal was similar to climbing a ladder, one rung at a time. Food was what their bodies cried out for, nourishment, the ability to rid their bodies of guilt and shame, hopelessness and fear, self-loathing and despair. Expulsion of feelings was replaced with the goodness of nutrition, health and well-being, with positive thoughts and actions.

Any discussion of food at the dinner table was forbidden. Playing with or cutting food into minute pieces was also taboo. They all had to be taught social skills, how to interact with other human beings. For support, a minimum of two caseworkers was present at each meal. Whatever was placed on the residents' dinner plates had to be eaten within the required 45 minutes. If a resident did not consume the entire meal during the allotted time, she was offered a container of Ensure, a nutritionally balanced supplemental drink.

That first night, Amy sat at the table and uncovered her dish, as did all the other residents. Mashed potatoes, red beets and an enormous chicken breast sat in front of her, waiting to be eaten. Instead, Amy's natural instinct of denial and avoidance made her talkative. The quiet one, speaker of few words, now began to chatter. She could not have eaten that food—her diversion was communication.

A social worker sitting next to Amy said words of encouragement, using therapeutic management to help Amy realize that the food was not her enemy. Amy began to cry. She no longer had complete solitude when she ate. All eyes at the table were on her. She could no longer hide. When the 45 minutes elapsed, Amy remained at the table. She had eaten only the potatoes, so she was given the Ensure as her supplement. She refused that, as well. Given the opportunity, she would have jumped out of that 20th story window.

After the girls assisted with the cleaning up, they entered the lounge for the next 45 minutes, where staff members monitored the residents' behaviors. This time was crucial for these women. With their thoughts so distorted about food and what its consumption meant to them, the staff's presence and counseling was imperative.

In the lounge, Amy met some of her fellow residents—Jen, Suzy, Stephanie, Kaylynn, Mary Ann, Michelle, Jean and Janis—just a few of the women with whom Amy would spend the next month, all residents, all suffering from eating disorders. Although each woman was complex and unique, they were united, for they all understood one another. Ranging in age from 14 to 28—the majority of the girls were in high school—these young women had taken a giant step in realizing they needed help. At age 32, Amy was the eldest resident and felt terribly out of place.

One young woman in particular, Michelle, made an impact on Amy. Severely emaciated, she seemed in a transient state. Her legs, ankles and feet retained fluid, swollen from laxative abuse, which had prevented her kidneys from functioning properly. Michelle took 100 laxatives per day, binged and purged and wanted to die. Her complexion was pallid, and she was a heavy smoker. She dressed fashionably; she loved to shop for clothing and accessories. She spoke very little. Amy knew Michelle was nearly invisible. They connected and became friends.

During her first two weeks, caseworkers monitored Amy very closely. Her condition, along with her depression, was considered critical. Amy tried to remain secluded in her room, but the social workers and staff would not allow it. Joann continued to take Amy to the dining room ten minutes before each meal, to show her what had been prepared for her. One evening at dinner, she observed Michelle, who sat to her right. Michelle's posture was perfectly poised and straight, her feet directly and evenly placed beneath her. As she sat in her trance-like demeanor, Amy saw and felt Michelle's legs trembling underneath the table and understood her terror. In that dining room, the girls discovered how exposed and vulnerable they were. One by one, they all became trancelike and robotic. *How strange*, Amy thought, and yet how perfectly understandable.

Thanksgiving, Hanukah and Christmas quickly approached, each holiday an anorexic's nightmare. Filled with joy, hustle and bustle for most people on earth, those on the 20th floor wanted to be as far removed as possible from anything resembling holiday cheer and the food that accompanied it. The night before Thanksgiving, the feast of the turkey, Amy thought of her mother and how she hated holidays and the preparation of the bird. She thought about how her father had treated his wife on those holidays, about his nasty remarks. For the first time, Amy realized why she despised such celebrations.

Amy spent Thanksgiving of 1990 with her temporary "new" family. At 11 that morning, the staff and residents at the Graduate Hospital joined a crowd downtown to watch the Thanksgiving Day Parade march down the streets of Philadelphia. The whole time, Amy's mind was on turkey. How was she going to get through the meal? The feast was celebrated at half past noon. Many of the girls went home on passes to spend the afternoon with their families, but at least half the residents sat at the dinner table. Amy ate the mashed potatoes and carrots. She did not touch the turkey. That afternoon, she talked with her husband and son on the phone; they were celebrating Thanksgiving dinner at Nanny's.

It was the longest day she spent on the unit. Still on Level I, Amy was not able to go outdoors unless a staff member was present, and on Thanksgiving Day, the floor was understaffed. She remained in her room most of the day.

On Friday, a major breakthrough occurred.

Black Friday Breakthrough

The extensive daily therapy was beginning to wear on Amy's sanity, scattering her thoughts and further confusing her. That night, after the Thanksgiving feast, she lay awake, thinking that her life was like a million-piece jigsaw puzzle, scattered on the floor before her, the box with the completed picture nowhere in sight. Surely the pieces must come together to form a whole picture, but she couldn't figure out how to make sense of the mess. She searched for clues, for answers, for some explanation that might help her begin to assemble the puzzle. She understood there was no simple answer, but rather a series of answers that somehow must make sense. She knew her problems began when she was a child, but had they developed over her life, inclusive of the present.? She needed to understand how the puzzle looked when it was completed—or she needed to find the corner pieces, the crux of the problem, and begin to lay the frame.

It was Black Friday, the day after Thanksgiving, and the official start of the holiday shopping season. That weekend, her husband and son were going to visit for the first time. She missed them terribly. Did they miss her? Was Jim Jr. adjusting? How was he doing at Nanny's and at school? She spoke with the two of them every day on the phone. Amy shed tears with her husband, but never let her son know how difficult her life was right now.

Up until then, Amy had not completed a single meal. The least stressful mealtime was breakfast; breakfast foods were safe for her—she did not know why. The first meal of the day was a breeze, but every meal thereafter was agony, filled with long minutes staring at a plate full of food she could not possibly eat. When the 45 minutes were up, Joann always brought Amy a glass of Ensure, but Amy had yet to taste it. She just couldn't bring herself to ingest the liquid.

On Black Friday, that night's dinner had been roasted pork, seasoned potatoes and squash, which she refused to try. Once again, she was detained; Joann sat next to Amy as she tried to drink the Ensure. The glass contained about six ounces. As Amy held the glass and sipped the drink, Joann spoke concerned, caring and positive words, asking Amy to gaze directly into her eyes and listen intently as Joann reminded her of the connection they had together. As Amy continued to try to drink the Ensure, Joann complimented Amy for her courage and endurance. She spoke of Amy's upcoming visit with her family on Sunday, how anxious and excited young Jim must be to see his mother. Joann talked about how James and Amy needed and loved one another, and how lucky Amy was to have her husband

and son in her life. As Amy continued to listen to Joann, never breaking eye contact, Amy managed to drink every drop of the Ensure! They grasped one another's hands—finally, a breakthrough! Amy smiled from ear to ear, and Joann was so pleased and proud of her. Amy had removed the first brink in the wall that surrounded her, and that first step proved to be a giant one. That day, Amy crossed her "eating barrier," regaining the ability to eat whatever meal she was served, without a tear or a flinch.

On Sunday morning, Amy eagerly awaited the boys' arrival. She had so much to tell them! Mother, husband and sun were overjoyed to see one another. Jim Jr. had brought his mother a stuffed dog dressed in a Santa suit and hat, something for her to snuggle with at bedtime. Amy had a four-hour pass for the afternoon, and they had plans for exploring the Natural Science and Dinosaur Museum after they had lunch at Friday's restaurant. Jim's two brothers and sister-in-law had also come along on the visit; they were astounded with her progress. The whole family toured the museum, snapping photographs, and then they walked around town before returning to the Windsor when Amy's four hours were up. It was difficult to say good-bye, but they'd be together the following Sunday and talk on the phone during the week.

On Monday mornings, Dr. Perry, the Graduate Hospital program director, and his team of doctors and nurses would evaluate each resident, discussing progression and eating plans and engaging in additional treatment and therapy. One by one, each patient would go to the conference room for her evaluation, often earning increased EP numbers and progressing to higher levels of the program. That Monday, Amy advanced to Level II, earning the privilege of selecting her own meals from the dietician's menu. She also gained the privilege to leave the unit with a Level III individual.

When Amy began to accept food, putting Level I behind her, she experienced a profound change, transforming from a severely depressed woman to an unrealistically euphoric and optimistic young woman. The lowest of lows went to the highest of highs. Was it the Prozac? Perhaps the doctors had been correct in diagnosing her with manic depression, a mental illness characterized by alternating periods of depression and mania. It became critical that she make everyone around her happy; she had to be certain that everyone liked and accepted her. She stopped in each resident's room, showering each of them with her euphoria, the fabrication that her ecstasy came from her breakthrough, and assuming that everyone else had to feel the same way. Some of the girls shunned her; others merely tolerated her. The "pleaser" had returned; this "good little girl" mindset, which reflected the opposite of her true self—so frightened inside—forced her to strive to become the "perfect patient." She followed every rule, mechanically completed every meal and persisted in serving her fellow residents with whatever she felt they needed.

At six o'clock each morning, the girls lined the hallway for weigh-in. Michelle and Kaylynn stood backward on the scale; others stood solemnly, staring straight ahead. After her breakthrough, Amy stepped onto the scale each morning feeling ecstatic, announcing her weight to all the girls, as well as the amount of weight she gained—as little as it was. She faithfully reported to her husband and family every day. Everything was wonderful and blissful, she thought. If she showed her cooperation and self-control, maybe she'd be granted an earlier discharge.

Amy was assigned an individual therapist. Three times a week, Amy met with her assigned therapist for individual treatment. They discussed many of the same issues Dr. Lora had broached in the previous months. Her therapist at the Graduate Hospital asked if Amy had ever been abused physically or sexually. In Amy's best recollection, she had not. However, Amy soon learned the meaning of the phrase "verbal abuse." Initially, she was surprised that there was a name for what had gone on in her household all throughout her childhood, but she came to understand that her father's parenting style was not normal or healthy.

Group therapy sessions, which included all the patients in the unit, also took place three times a week. The group objective was to unite the girls and encourage them to interact with one another. They were all in a crisis; group sessions made them aware that they were not alone in their struggle. Each session, the therapist chose at random someone to begin; when it was Amy's turn, all she wanted to do was run out of the room. When she realized she couldn't flee, she wept. She hated being under the microscope.

In weekly family therapy, the goal was to educate the resident's family about her eating disorder—family therapy was not about perpetuating ill feelings, pointing fingers or assigning blame to anyone. Amy believed that if her father had been alive, he'd boldly tell her to just sit down and eat. He would not have accepted or understood her disorder. On the other hand, most members of Amy's family sacrificed one day of work for her. Amy apologized to them; in her mind she was not worth the trip to Philadelphia. However, family therapy helped her realize these discussions were invaluable to all of them. During the sessions, her siblings denounced their father, while her mother consistently blamed herself. With Amy and her family all in one room together, ill feelings resurfaced, often causing one or more of the family members to erupt with anger or frustration. Whenever this happened, Amy wished she had the power to snap her fingers and disappear. She felt as though everything was her fault, that there was no hope for her situation.

When time allowed after their family therapy, Amy received a pass outside for an hour. Sensing everyone's uneasiness, Amy usually suggested they walk to the park and talk about other topics. Not once did she eat out with them during these breaks; it was exhausting enough that she was spending the time working out their problems. Communication was critical to her recovery, and it was a new skill for all of them; it had never existed in their home. She felt uneasy and nervous with her family, just as she always felt at the dinner table during her first week at the Windsor.

Art therapy helped the residents express themselves through drawings, when it seemed too difficult to speak freely about troubling emotions and ideas. During one of her sessions, Amy drew a picture of herself and her mother sitting together in her mother's kitchen. High-backed antique chairs surrounded the oval, antique-oak table, which her father had hand-stripped and refinished to its original beauty. In the drawing, Amy sat at one end of the table, with her mother at the other. Dozens of bubbled captions filled the page, each of her mother's major and minor life dilemmas written inside the bubbles—negative, depressive thoughts, ideas and sentences, all of which flowed in Amy's direction and filled her, every one, one on top of the other. Amy never responded to any of the thoughts that engulfed her, just absorbed them. Her mother released her negativity and depression, and Amy held it trapped within her for years. Recharged so frequently with all that negativity, she did not know how to deal with it all. She released some of the anxiety on her husband, usually unloading her feelings of anger toward her mother, which caused unpleasant feelings and bitterness to affect Amy's marriage.

In another drawing, one of the therapists asked Amy to lie down on the floor, on top of a life-sized piece of brown packaging paper, while the therapist traced the outline of Amy's body. Amy stood up and looked at the tracing, which the therapist held upright, and relayed her perceptions of the drawing. Amy saw a ghost-like figure, obscure and unidentifiable—that was her, barely there. She was so close to invisibility. Her therapist asked questions about Amy's feeling about the sketch, and afterward, they rolled up the tracing and placed a rubber band around it. When Amy was discharged, the drawing was given to her. She hid the picture in her attic, wondering from time to time if it was still there or if her husband had thrown it away.

Movement therapy and psychodrama were two other types of therapy. Amy disliked both. In movement therapy, the residents moved their bodies to rhythm and motion while music played. This therapy was designed to help the girls become more aware of their bodies as objects in space and to help them accept themselves as human beings. Believing she was uncoordinated, Amy always felt her lack of grace during movement therapy. She was embarrassed to have the other women watch her. Psychodrama was center stage, drama and role-playing performed without a written script. Participation in this therapy was minimal—the last place those girls wanted to be was in front of the other residents, giving a performance.

Once a week, the staff presented the residents with three choices for social activity outside the unit, letting the women decide which event to attend. The first week Amy was there, they walked to the theater to see *Home Alone*, starring McCauley Caulkin, the conniving ten-year-old left behind when his family vacationed for the Christmas holiday. Amy, exhausted from her therapies that day, dozed for a bit in the movie theater. She must have been subconsciously listening, though, because the film and its soundtrack remained embedded in Amy's mind.

The second week featured a panoramic movie extravaganza. When the film began, the visual and sound effects were so intense that Amy felt as though she was up on the screen, seated in the front row of a roller coaster. The experience made her feel dizzy and queasy. Unable to watch it, she kept her eyes tightly shut throughout the movie's entirety, feigning sleep and praying for the movie to end. Lighter activities included visiting the shopping mall, seeing a play, *The Christmas Story*, and a night spent in the lounge, watching rented movies. Amy loved the movie-rental night; indoors, in one room together, all the residents snoozed on the floor, most falling asleep halfway through the video rentals. Amy felt a wonderful sense of togetherness, imagining that teenaged slumber parties must have been like this night.

The ultimate adventure was the time Amy rode the Philadelphia subway to see her first NBA basketball game: the Philadelphia 76er's vs. the San Antonio Spurs. Before the game, the group had a dinner of fish, rice pilaf, salad and dessert. Amy felt stuffed! They left the Graduate Hospital and walked a few blocks to the subway. Although Amy felt anxious and nervous, she didn't discuss her feelings with one of the caseworkers that accompanied them. The group went down a short stairway, underground, and awaited the arrival of the subway. When it arrived, the women moved to the rear of the subway, and the train quickly began to move, zipping along the tracks. Feeling the sensation that they were moving backward, not forward, Amy thought of the fish she had for dinner and felt sick to her stomach.

She tried to keep her mind off of her stomach by chatting with the woman sitting next to her, and in no time at all, the subway halted. *Thank God in Heaven,* she thought. She was pleased that she hadn't become physically sick in the subway.

Once inside the Spectrum, they found their seats, located in "peanut heaven," as they say. Rich, Amy's mental-health technician, sat in the seat next to her. She felt uncomfortable with him so close by, worried that he thought Amy needed constant supervision during the event. She knew that part of his job that night was to observe and evaluate her behavior. She didn't know if it was the proximity of the caseworker or her anxiety at being in a stadium filled with so many other people, but she wasn't able to concentrate, and she watched the basketball game with indifference. Looking around at one point, she saw that although the depressed residents of the 20th floor were trying their best to be socially active, it seemed difficult for most of them. The return subway trip was not as terrifying, but Amy was relieved to be back on the unit.

She continued to make progress. When December began, Amy started to keep a daily journal; her first entry was dated 12-04-90. To help her manage her struggle and despair, her therapist had suggested Amy write down her feelings, thoughts and questions. Her journal writing caused a number of long-buried feelings to resurface; she awoke one night feeling so disturbed that she sought a counselor's help. She had dreamed of her father. He had always told her mother to keep the family together, no matter what. Her mother had not kept his wish; instead, she pushed her family away. Amy had tried desperately to help her mother battle her depression and to provide support to everyone around her—which, of course meant excluding herself. She spent a long time talking to the counselor that night, another small step forward for Amy, and this new ability to ask for help when she needed it.

Amy continued to eat all her meals, gain weight and hold onto her happy frame of mind. Later, after she left the hospital, she realized how obnoxious she must have appeared to the other women. Everyone was so depressed—sad, withdrawn, pale and emaciated—while Amy tried hard to be the perfect patient. As she continued to gain weight, Amy thought she was doing what she was supposed to be doing, getting better. She was eating, so the therapy and treatment must have helped her. Yet she didn't understand why she seemed so much happier and energetic than the other women who had reached or surpassed her level of recovery. Had someone cast a spell on her? Had she been hypnotized and ordered to feel so delighted? Were all of the residents transformed into robots? What had happened there, on that eating disorder unit?

The holidays were quickly approaching, and Amy wasn't scheduled to leave until December 20. Thank goodness she had completed most of her Christmas shopping while she was still at home! Each night, she crossed off the date on the calendar by her bed. She longed to see her boys. Each Sunday brought a new experience for them—they'd enjoy lunch together at a restaurant, followed by another exciting museum tour. There were so many things to see in Philadelphia! At home, whenever they ate out it was always at a fast-food restaurant, where Amy either ordered a drink or had nothing at all. During these outings from the Windsor, she progressed each week and made moderate changes. She began to feel good about herself.

An outpouring of mail arrived daily, beginning the second week she was on the unit: cards of encouragement, get-well greetings, notes and letters came from her family and friends. Reading so many kind words and prayers, she was touched by the people who had taken the time to send her a card or letter. She had never realized the support she already had back home. James, her charmer, sent a dozen red roses to the unit each week, and friends often sent flower arrangements, too.

In group therapy one afternoon, one of the women said that she envied Amy. "Please" Amy replied, "do not envy me." Amy had been taught never to envy anyone; envy was a sin. The counselor said that envy was an emotion, a true feeling. It was completely normal to feel envious of another person and perfectly acceptable to feel the emotion. That day, Amy learned to accept feelings she'd been taught were wrong. It marked the beginning of her acceptance of who she was and the eating disorder from which she suffered.

Letter writing became a part of her daily routine. On paper, she was able to explain to her three nieces why she was in Philadelphia, so that they could have a clearer concept of the crisis out of which she was fighting her way. Her nieces were almost teenagers, and Amy worried that they, too, could become susceptible to an eating disorder. Amy also wrote to her mentor and second mother, Theresa, whom she had not contacted for a few years. She knew that even though their relationship had been distant during the last few years of torment and decline, Theresa cared about her very much. In quiet moments, Amy wrote, thought, searched and questioned, using her journal to explore her own mind. She continued to look for clues, for answers, as well for missing pieces of her puzzling life.

Residents departed, and new girls arrived. Amy reached Level III, becoming proctor for several Level I and Level II residents. She invited Michelle to go out to the mall, and they shopped for an hour, treating themselves to clothes, jewelry and makeup. On another occasion, a few of the girls made appointments at a nearby salon. A "new do" lifted their spirits, self-confidence and self-worth. These were small pleasures, treasures that boosted further along their road to recovery.

The girls decorated the dining room and doorways for Christmas and Hanukah. Janis was Jewish and introduced Amy to a few of her family's customs and traditions. An artificial tree added festivity to the lounge, and the women exchanged a gift with one another. Janis presented Amy with a small, purple dreidel for Amy to keep as a reminder of their friendship. The mood in the lounge was solemn that evening, even with the tree lighting up the corner of the room. They all seemed saddened. Amy thought that holiday celebrations must have been unhappy times for all the women. It reflected in their faces.

The weeks counted down to days, and Amy looked forward to and prepared for her release from the unit. James told her that he and Jim were anxiously crossing off the days on their calendar, too.

December 20 was drawing near. On the last weekend Amy spent on the floor, several women gave her "goodbye" gifts. She received a lovely barrette and pin from Jean. A few days prior to her discharge, Amy needed to read, understand and sign a number of forms. The hospital's After-Care Plan," four pages long, stated her admission and discharge dates, her home therapist's name and address and the recommendation that she continue therapy with Dr. Lora once a week and attend a weekly group session, if available. The second page listed daily medications and described an exercise program that consisted of a one-to-two mile walk every other day. She was to continue at her current eating level, EP9, keeping mealtimes limited to 45 minutes and making sure a support person was present. She should also spend 45 minutes after each meal "cooling off," as she'd done at the Graduate Hospital. If necessary, Amy could ask for support from her family.

Her ideal weight was listed as 130 lbs., plus or minus 10%, which sounded astronomical to her. She never weighed that much in her life! The After-Care Plan's final directive was for her to find part-time employment within two months of her discharge. Amy felt uneasy. What would happen if she did not consent to this recommendation? Would she be hospitalized again? She had to do everything that they told her. She had to be perfect. If she did any less, she would be worthless.

The third page of the After-Care Plan further discussed the part-time job recommendation, suggesting she find a non-stressful, part-time job. She was also supposed to increase her socialization with friends and attend planned outings once a week. The plan addressed Amy's personal comments about her treatment and tried to anticipate any problems she may have adhering to the plan, giving ideas for coping with them. The final page asked for Amy's signature, which indicated that she understood and would participate in her aftercare treatment.

Upon discharge, each patient received a notebook, cleverly designed and assembled by the occupational and art therapists. On the cover of Amy's notebook was a tiny, whimsical, cute-looking critter. The notebook itself was an autograph album, a keepsake that held words of encouragement and well wishes from the staff, residents and caseworkers. Included were the addresses and telephone numbers of the women, so that they could keep in touch after they were all back home. She snapped photos to include in the book; using a camera James brought Amy on one of his visits.

During those thirty days at the Graduate Hospital on the 20th floor of the Windsor Hotel, Amy endured a difficult time in her life, emerging victorious on the other side. She had learned to give and to receive a warm-hearted hug, embraces that were truly meaningful, gestures of affection that showed that someone loved and cared about her, and she for them. Only later, years after her hospitalization, Amy realized that she had touched people's hearts during her 30-day stay. She continued to help others throughout her lifetime; the ability was always within her, but she had needed the Graduate Hospital to unlock it.

On the night of December 19, 1990, Amy carefully packed her belongings. The next day, she was going home.

Homecoming

On December 20, 1990, Amy awoke at five in the morning. Her six o'clock weigh-in showed she weighed 100 pounds. Realizing she was out of danger, Amy felt proud. However, she was apprehensive about leaving the unit. What would life be like without the continual assistance and daily therapy? She wasn't looking forward to saying good-bye to everyone. A special bond and commitment united these young women. What did their futures hold? Would they succeed in piecing their lives together? Would they gain confidence and move forward? Although she was prepared to take on new challenges, Amy still needed assurance about her future.

Jim and her brother, Eric, arrived around 11:00 A.M. One by one, she said farewell to her friends, embracing them as they wiped away tears. They promised to write, but Amy didn't imagine she'd ever see any of these women again. This thought made her feel sad. That special group of girls understood one another. "What type of lives would they lead?" Amy wondered. The only reason she'd known them was because she'd been at the Windsor. She certainly wasn't going to be back! After saying goodbye to Joann, Amy, James and Eric walked toward the elevator and took Amy's final ride down from the 20th floor.

The two-hour car ride home was peaceful. Eric drove while James and Amy talked, laughed and made a few plans for the day. Little James was at school, and when Amy's dear friend, Rose, dropped him off at home, Amy planned to thank her for her kindness, concern, love and support; while Amy was at the Windsor, Rose had transported her son to and from school each day. Coincidentally, that day was Rose's birthday; in future years, Amy always associated her friend's birthday with her discharge from the Graduate Hospital.

In what seemed like no time, they were back in town. Eric drove up Center Street, parking in front of Amy and James's home. After they unloaded Amy's things, she hugged her brother, thanked him and told him how much she loved him. She was finally home. She couldn't wait to get inside!

When she opened the front door, she was astonished to see that James and Jim Jr. had already decorated for Christmas. The tree was beautiful! Hung between their two sitting rooms was a banner that read, "Welcome Home, Mom!" It reminded her of the banner she had designed when her father had come home from the hospital. They stood beneath it and embraced. They had missed each other so much; they hadn't spent this much time apart since before they'd met. They kissed with great passion, knowing their love for each other was forever.

When the couple came back to reality, they realized that they needed to stock the cupboards and refrigerator with groceries. After going shopping at their local supermarket, they came home and ate lunch together. Amy was very conscious of the number of proteins, starches, lipids, fruits and milk she needed to fulfill her Eating Plan number for the day, and she felt almost excited about meeting her goal for lunch. After lunch, they spent long-awaited intimate time together. God had given this gift to Amy, her husband, whom she loved endlessly. He was the most giving, caring, loving man on the earth. He had sacrificed so much for her. During their time together that afternoon, Amy remembered why: His love for her was as deep as the love she felt for him.

Later, they walked hand-in-hand to her mother-in-law's home, six blocks away, enjoying the brisk December air. Amy felt alive again. Still feeling exuberant from her long rest at the Windsor, Amy reminded herself to remain positive, express herself and be a good wife and mother. She'd ask for help; she'd find a job. She would continue to be kind to herself. She was a good person, and she mattered to others in this world. She was worthwhile! To stay healthy, she knew she needed to reinforce herself constantly with positive thoughts.

James would support her, as would his mother and family. Perhaps they did not fully comprehend her disorder, but she knew she could rely on them. Amy's older siblings offered strength and encouragement, and her younger brothers would help her as best they could. As for her mother, well, Amy could only hope for the best. Her mother had sent her a card in the hospital that said she did not know how to help Amy. Although Amy knew her faith in God and prayer would help her find healing through her doctors; Amy searched for something more from her mother, the hope that her mother would try a little harder to be more positive herself. Amy yearned for her mother to look honestly at Amy and tell her she cared for her, to give a hug that felt like a hug, not like a gesture of duty.

Amy's mother had needed psychotherapy and antidepressants for more than 30 years, but Amy's father would never allow that. In those days, depression was considered a flaw in one's character; the individual was weak and imperfect if she showed any signs of mental illness. It was thought that depression was a choice, not a disease; therefore, no one had a remedy for it, no advice other than, "cheer up." Like mother, like daughter—maybe once, but no longer. Unlike her mother, Amy chose to seek help from outside sources. She could not fight these feelings alone and live a meaningful life for herself and her family. She had chosen to become a better person, to become different from her mother. But she knew she had to take small strides: Many ups and downs lay ahead.

When she saw her daughter-in-law, Nanny's first words were, "God bless you, Amy," and she welcomed her daughter-in-law with outstretched arms and a gentle, heartfelt hug. Nan was always in her kitchen, cooking and preparing meals, baking one of her delightful recipes, or upstairs, in her beauty shop, taking care of her patrons.

Sociable, loving, generous and often demanding, Nan was always there for Amy and her family. She welcomed her son and grandson whenever they came over, cooked for them, washed their clothing and got them off to work and school. When she needed help, she asked for it. Family and a network of friends were by her side. She practiced Little Jim's prayers with him, helped him with his schoolwork and practiced his speech lessons the school's speech therapist assigned. She prayed her rosary and made novenas. She gave of herself ceaselessly to those she dearly loved. Nan believed in herself as a woman and a mother; she loved who she was, and, in turn, loved all those around her.

James, Amy and Nanny sat around the kitchen table, chatting as they waited for Rose's Explorer to pull into the driveway, bringing Jim Jr. home from school. When he finally arrived, Amy had an armful of fresh flowers ready when she stepped onto the front porch to greet him. The sight of her son was a balm to her soul. What a joyful reunion it was! Her son was now on Christmas break; she would enjoy his company all day long for the next two weeks.

Christmas was in only five days. Excitement was in the air as Amy hurried with last minute shopping and gift-wrapping. Whenever she felt as though the preparations might be too overwhelming for her, Amy reminded herself that she was back in the real world again, and the real world was a busy, hectic place, especially just before the holidays. She was determined to move ahead.

Her first challenge was Christmas Eve dinner at her mother's house. Her sister, Susan, flew in from California to visit Amy and the family, which made the meal more enjoyable. Christmas day came and went, with loads of presents for everyone. Somehow, Amy survived the holidays in one piece. However, without the Graduate Hospital's constant structure and support Amy had received from her caseworkers, she noticed she was a little uncomfortable at dinnertime. The doctors had told her to expect such discomfort during her first few weeks home. Things would improve once Amy found her support team at home.

Amy remained on the "Windsor High" for weeks after her discharge, returning to daily responsibilities with an almost-euphoric attitude. She continued to work in her journal, writing down several New Year's resolutions for 1991. She resumed therapy with Dr. Lora in early January, continuing to take Prozac. When she talked with Dr. Lora, Amy was relieved to find that she felt comfortable and was able to talk through her anxiety. Dr. Lora listened, guided and advised Amy, as they worked together to increase Amy's self-confidence and emotional stamina. After the New Year began, she made her first job-hunt efforts, sending out resumes and cover letters to ten established businesses in her area. She was nervous about entering the workplace again, but she knew how important it was for her to find a low-stress part-time job. She received a call in February to interview for a part-time position in a dental office, as an assistant for a dentist opening a practice in Kingston, a town eight miles from Amy's home. Amy accepted the job, and began in March of 1991. Amy's hours were one o'clock to nine o'clock, two days a week. On those days, Jim Jr. went to Nanny's after school. Amy had previous knowledge and experience in dental procedures, which made her feel somewhat comfortable. She was excited; hopeful the job would help her reposition her thoughts.

Amy had only been out of the eating disorder unit a few short weeks when she discovered she was beginning to regress. Who required her to sit at the dinner table for 45 minutes and offered her Ensure if she were unable to finish her meal? Certainly, James did not—as her husband, he was there to support her, but he did not want to act like her caseworker or therapist. On some days, she did not fulfill her required caloric intake, which caused her to feel a great deal of guilt. But her family needed her as a wife and a mother. Was it even possible for her to accept her responsibilities, learn from her past experiences, remain healthy and grow beyond the limits of her eating disorder?

When a woman takes on the job of becoming a mother, she is also rewarded with many additional professions: a 24-hour caretaker, nurse, nurturer, teacher, disciplinarian, interpreter and artist. She becomes a comedian, a connoisseur, a night owl, a nightwalker, an elf, an athlete, the Easter Bunny and the Tooth Fairy. She mends torn clothing and hurt feelings. She's a believer and a receiver. She is a gift of love to her husband and children, someone who must remember to care for herself, even if she is selfless. Motherhood is a difficult job, all performed with only on-the-job training. She remembered the words that her father-in-law had said to her years ago. A mother's heart enlarges, and not in cardiac arrest; from infant into toddler, from school age to adolescence and adult, a child gives his mother bits and pieces of love, all of which increase a mother's heart and soul. She experiences the first time an infant opens his eyes, the first smiles, laughs and words, from crawling to first steps, and then to climbing, the first time riding a two-wheeler and the months when their smile is toothless. Before we realize it, children are in kindergarten, meeting new friends. James and Amy held gala birthday parties and spent exhausting Christmas Eves assembling toys. They entered the sacraments of First Holy Communion and Confirmation and supported the teachings of their faith. Middle school and part-time jobs would lead to a driver's license and graduation from high school. Amy's heart grew larger each day with a glance, a word, the sounds of laughter—and, best of all, the way Jim Jr. treated others, respecting them as he respected himself.

Throughout all this goodness, all these precious moments, Amy thanked God for her son and husband each and every day. Outwardly, she was happy and grateful. Inwardly, however, she still questioned her ability and to have self-destructive thoughts. Life was difficult and stressful, and the demon returned, the creature within her that demanded she destroy herself a little more each day with rituals and obsessive-compulsive behaviors. The war continued. Amy was blessed with so many wonderful attributes, and yet she still searched for greater things.

The next troublesome piece in Amy's puzzle was perfection. Although perfection is, of course, impossible to achieve, the stuff of fairy tales, dreams and make-believe, she tried desperately to make everything flawless: her home, her job, her relationships with family and friends, any special projects or plans. If something was less than perfect, Amy became anxious and upset, overcome with anger and fright. Focused and fixated on an impossible ideal, she nevertheless strived for it, refusing to accept worry, disappointment and sadness, all emotions with which she had immense difficulty dealing, and continuing to punish herself for her feelings of inadequacy.

Within three months, Amy's weight reached 109 lbs. She had gained 19 pounds since the day she'd been hospitalized, and she began to panic! The scale never reached 110. Her journal entrees became more negative, and she restricted her diet a little more each day. Amy formed a new group of "safe foods." Jim attempted time and time again to be supportive, but began to struggle and became frustrated with her. Intervals of "block out" time returned, and she began to shut her husband out once again. She felt herself slowly sinking further into depression, even though Jim tried hard to keep her above water. The dreadful feelings returned; she awoke at night numerous times, experiencing guilt for failing to follow her doctors' instructions. What a failure she was as a human being. She could not lie; the scale always told the truth. This was the time when she needed to ask and accept support from her family. She chose not to. She was embarrassed by her behavior.

A small part of her kept fighting. She changed her appearance, using the rationale that if she was well enough to care about how she looked; then she was perfectly fine. She remembered Michelle, from the 20th floor, an attractive woman with very short blonde hair and multiple ear piercings. Amy had her hair cut off, into a short style, but she decided to let her ears alone. Never once did Amy connect the woman she idolized with the woman's true self—"near death" Michelle, who had spent additional weeks in the hospital because of her critical condition and failure to thrive.

As he had before, Jim Jr. was tuned into his mother's anxieties. Children are very perceptive little people and learn favorable and unfavorable qualities from their parents. As tension between her and James escalated, it affected Jim Jr. Amy wanted to go back in time, to when she and James were younger and carefree, to a time when the sun always seemed to shine. She did not want to be an adult; she was not ready.

Two personalities lived within her, constantly conflicted and festering: One fought to die; one fought to live.

Return to the Working World

March 5, 1991, was Amy's first day at her new job. The dentist had joined his father's practice and needed another assistant for fourhanded dentistry, a dental technique that allows the dentist and dental assistant to work as a team, seated in front of the patient. Dr. Anthony was a pleasant, intelligent and informative man and was soon to be married. Amy admired his personality and felt very comfortable working with him. Also employed in the office were a receptionist and his father's assistant.

As the practice saw patients during the afternoons and evenings, as well as two Saturday mornings a month, Amy eventually took on the additional responsibilities of a front-office receptionist. She learned how to work a computer and distribute electronic insurance claims forms. When a nearby community college offered a class for radiography certification, Dr. Anthony encouraged her to attend and get certified at the practice's expense. Amy received a very honorable grade on the exam, which authorized her to take dental radiographs. She was pleased with her performance in the class and on the exam. It was a positive experience in the morass of uncertainty and self-doubt that continued to plague her.

She felt a high after passing the exam that was similar to how she felt after she "graduated" from the Graduate Hospital. As a result, she began to expand her social and professional life. She accepted the receptionist's lunch invitation one day and spent a pleasant hour chatting with her as they ate at a corner delicatessen. On another evening, Amy attended an optional staff meeting that outlined new dental procedures and sterilization techniques; she also attended an

American Heart Association CPR course. When she returned home after her work each day, she actually had conversations with Jim, sharing with him stories about the different patients she encountered and skills she was learning. Finally, she had a meaningful focal point outside her home that gave her satisfaction, something besides housework and mothering to discuss. She was beginning to feel worthwhile and her confidence level heightened.

Amy's most difficult social challenge was attending a dinner conference for local dentists, their office staff and associates. She was anxious and worried about what the evening would entail. What would she be required to eat? Would she be able to eat it all? Would she be able to remain relaxed and make conversation with the people around her? She had made outstanding progress at work thus far— she was trying! She was making small steps, returning into the world of the living a bit at a time, but she needed to prove to herself that she was a capable, competent and efficient employee. She attended the social function, ate most of the dinner and had pleasant conversation with the people seated next to her.

As was the case before, when she was first married and outwardly happy, the positive aspects of her life outweighed the negative. And then, again, the negative took its turn. Food restriction became easier on the days she worked: She and the doctor were sometimes so busy with patients that there was little or no time for her to eat supper. No one knew except Amy, and her anorexia would never let her tell. She began to fall further into depression, suffering from agonizing bouts of self-doubt, convinced of her own inadequacy.

James became emotionally exhausted with his wife, struggling over the best way to help her. He talked with her about their joint session with Dr. Lora last November, reminding her of her competency as a wife and mother, but she refused to acknowledge the truth of his words. Finally, at a loss about how to proceed, he made a mistake: In the state of Pennsylvania, he had the legal right to take Jim away from her. He decided to frighten her into recovery by threatening to leave her and take James with him. She broke down in tears, almost hysterical, until Jim relented and revealed that he had only been trying to help understand what she could lose if she continued to destroy herself.

Therapy with Dr. Lora continued, with Amy agonizing before each session and keeping her participation in these sessions to a minimum. Finally, in April, Dr. Lora had enough of Amy's behavior. The doctor told Amy to accept her responsibilities or her husband would leave her soon. She told Amy either to make the changes and grow up, or to stop wasting both their time and her money on therapy. "I am not your mother!" Dr. Lora said, refusing to be responsible for Amy's decision-making. The doctor also said Amy had made little, if any, progress since her hospitalization. The doctor concluded the session by suggesting she take a break in therapy until she was ready to try again, reiterating that she would be there for her when the time came. After crying the entire hour of the appointment, Amy left the office, humiliated, devastated by what had happened. She discontinued her sessions.

Dr. Lora had spoken the truth. Amy had cooperated at the unit and done as she was told, improving so she could gain her release. After she came home, she stopped trying. Although she had found the job she'd been required to get, she'd never established the critical support system she needed to grow and thrive. She needed Dr. Lora for a weekly "pep talk," because there was no one who could physically make her eat. Recruiting a meal partner was too difficult a task for Amy. She was the loner, the outcast, incapable of asking another person to give her this level of help. A part of Amy felt relieved that Dr. Lora had released her from her care. Amy needed time to think for herself and decide how she was going to live her life.

She revisited her journal writing. It became a method of freedom when face-to-face conversation was impossible. She could no longer keep secrets locked inside her and found an outlet for her feelings on paper, writing letters to the people in her life. The first person she wrote to was her mother. Ironically, she wrote the letter in May, the month in which Mother's Day was celebrated. Amy wrote eight pages of genuine feelings about the past and present. When she finished, she hesitated a few days, afraid to give the letter to her mother. Surely, her mother would be angry and refuse to speak with Amy. One day, while her mother was at work, Amy snuck into the house and placed the letter on her mother's kitchen table. Days passed without a word from her. As she'd predicted, Amy had to take control of the situation and approach her mother first.

That Saturday morning, she and little James walked the five blocks to her childhood home. On their way, they stopped at the floral shop and bought a bouquet of carnations, her mother's favorite flower. When they arrived, Jim presented the gift to his grandmother. Amy thought the fresh flowers would break the ice. They visited for a while, and then ventured home, not a word spoken about the letter.

Later that day, Amy went back to her mother's house, alone. They talked about what Amy had written and cried together, but Amy knew that her mother was not about to change very much. Unless she herself made the change, Amy was fated to be the daughter that ended up by her mother's side, consoling her over the littlest heartbreak. Amy needed to accept her mother as she was and initiate the changes in herself. Amy vowed to help her when she was able, but keep her own family as her first priority. If she wanted to save her family, she had no other choice.

That first year after her stay at the Hotel Windsor, life was an emotional roller coaster. Years later, Amy realized how emotionally abusive she had been to her husband and son. Her husband, so strong and easy-going, so handsome, remained by Amy's side, picking her up each time she fell down. For better and for worse, he held his vows, no matter how difficult she made it; he loved her that much. Each time Amy's depression and obsessions overwhelmed her, these behaviors affected her son. Young Jim's night-fright episodes returned. He never remembered his dreams or the way he acted when he had them; his body and subconscious mind responded to her dysfunctional behavior. Later, when she was finally able to realize how bad things were during those dark years, Amy regretted the way she had mistreated her family. Her boys meant the world to her.

Amy knew she had made some small success: she'd succeeded with her goal of being functional in the working world. While she was at Dr. Anthony's office, her mind was occupied with other priorities; she engaged in intellectual activity rather than concentrating totally on food all day long. It was a beginning; she was a competent human being. Somewhere inside her were hidden treasures, the qualities of goodness and love. She had to find and release them. At age 32, Amy was ready to wipe the slate clean and start fresh. She wasn't the only person in the world who was suffering; how many other individuals had endured trauma, been abused or abandoned or lost loved ones? Millions. Amy wasn't the only person to experience hardship, and all those other people had found a way to live again. All human beings needed to learn, cope and deal with life's hardships and disappointments, and so would she. She began her journey.

In July of that summer, Amy made another appointment with Dr. Lora. Amy felt so bad when the doctor had confronted her during their last session, and yet she had found enough strength inside her to go on. As Dr. Lora had promised, she was there for Amy.

After that session, instead of turning her stress inward, Amy tried to rethink the circumstance or situation and find a way to deal with it without feeling self-destructive. A stressful experience did not have to become Amy's problem alone. If a loved one experienced difficulties or sorrow, that did not mean Amy had to feel those same emotions. Her family confided in her because they trusted her—she was "the listener," available whenever anyone needed her—but she didn't have to respond emotionally to the burdens they unloaded on her. She learned to look out for what was best for her, what made her feel comfortable. In regards to her mother, she kept a safe distance. She asked other siblings to help out, instead of letting her mother treat her as her caretaker. Amy was capable of making decisions. She took care of herself, for a change.

Not every day was a good day; she still needed to have control over her body and continued to weigh herself in the morning and evening. As she read what she had written in her journal, she saw that the numbers were continuing to dwindle: 105 pounds dropped to 101 and, by October, 100 pounds. Amy considered herself halfway rehabilitated, split into two: 50% moved forward, 50% backward.

In mid October, she felt comfortable enough to discontinue her therapy. Dr. Lora had done all that she could for Amy. The time came for Amy to handle her life without Dr. Lora. She gradually weaned herself from the Prozac. Was that the correct path?

Something pleasant happened over the holidays. Amy's sister, Susan, from California, bred her female lhasa apso; her "Snuggles" delivered six puppies in early September. She sold them one by one, when the pups were old enough, keeping two behind. Susan planned to keep one of the pups, but she had asked Amy earlier if she wanted to have one from the litter. At first, Amy was skeptical and hesitant, never having gotten over her experience with Dusty. She and James declined. Then when Susan telephoned in December and relayed that the first-born puppy, black and white in color, was the sole puppy left, Amy melted and asked James if it was possible to take the pup. He relented, and the pup became a Christmas gift for little Jim. This time, Amy was determined to find information and resources that could assist her with training the puppy. She missed the companionship of a dog. She felt mature and confident that she could take on the additional responsibility. The puppy brought joy to Jim, and that made Amy very happy.

They had to think of a clever name for this California canine. Susan named hers Amelia, and Amy came up with Abigail, or Abbey, for short. On December 20, via TWA, Susan arrived with Snuggles, Amelia and Abbey. Everyone met at Amy's mother's house, where her sister stayed over the holidays.

It was always special when Susan came home. She lived across the country and visits were few and far between. The house bustled with the three dogs and their mother's beagle, Spot. Amelia and Abbey were tiny balls of fur, and young Jim could not keep up with them. They took Abbey home with them that evening.

Abbey was a spirit lifter. Amy and her son loved animals, and

Abbey's playfulness and spunk was therapeutic for her. A good job, a new puppy and young Jim beside himself with excitement all made that Christmas a merry one.

Amy worked on her attitude with her mother. With her sister home for a short time, Amy knew Susan would be the receptor of her mother's negativity; for a short time, Amy had a break. Unfortunately, she also had time to dwell upon her own problems. Guilt lay heavily on her. The lies, the hiding, her eating habits, all weighed her down. After 30 days at the Windsor, a year ago, she still played the game. She'd take two steps forward, and then two back. In January of 1992, she weighed 97 pounds. Was it withdrawal from the antidepressant? As she struggled, she became defensive, forgetting to put herself in her husband's position and realize how much she was hurting him. He again endured the slow process of losing his wife, the first and only girl with whom he had fallen in love. He tried desperately to understand her. He was patient; she treated him terribly.

Every emotion Amy had failed to express in her youth, she tested with Jim. He allowed her to release these feelings on him, and he always forgave her. He loved her and sacrificed himself for her, and yet she was blind to his love when she was behind that wall of her own making. Each time he blasted through her protective confinement, he released his wife. She always apologized for how she had acted, so sorry for the pain she caused Jim while she dwelt in that place of darkness and despair.

From Christmas break until March of 1992, Jim Jr. developed a phobia about going to school. He cried and complained of stomach upset every morning, which caused Amy distress, as well. A few times, when Amy dropped him off at the school's entrance, he'd come back out of the building, running toward her as she walked to her car. She'd take him back inside to his first-grade classroom. He'd scream and cry, but he'd stay in class. Was it holiday back-to-school blues, Amy's two-day-a-week job or the new puppy that was making him feel so insecure? Did he miss his Mom and Abbey? Soon enough, spring arrived, and they looked forward to the end of the school year.

Memories and a New Life

Throughout 1992, Mrs. Montgomery visited her doctors more frequently, suffering from allergies and asthma, high blood pressure, bursitis, diverticulitis, gout, cataracts, arthritis and depression. She had to fill numerous prescriptions and take a handful of pills each day, also using inhalants for her asthmatic condition. The task of ferrying their mother back and forth from the doctors' offices alternated between Ann and Amy. Frustrated by her failing health, their mother contemplated retiring from the bank.

Spring came and Amy sighed. She loved the springtime, the sounds of birds in the morning, the buds erupting on the trees, warmer temperatures, spring cleaning and the pleasure of opened windows for much-awaited fresh air. From what she had learned at the hospital, Amy guessed that she was experiencing seasonal affective disorder, a depressive mood disorder associated with seasonal variations of light. Her spirits and general mood lifted when there was more daylight.

Summer soon followed, with the thrill of no homework, books or studies. It was always a pleasure to be freed from schedules and routines. For a few months, Amy felt relaxed and rejuvenated, but she soon felt worried again when it came time to get ready for the annual trip to Canada. The week spent at the lake was always memorable; yet Amy felt the same panic each summer, as she procrastinated about packing, making too many to-do lists, waffling over what to bring and struggling to make everything fit in their car.

Although her anxiety manifested during her preparations, she knew the real problem was with the negative emotions and memories she associated with the cabin and her father. Five years had passed since his death, and she still had unresolved issues. As they neared the cottage, her anxious state peaked. She was glad to return to their family retreat, but she found it difficult being surrounded by so many memories of her father.

Her father's picture sat on a hand-carved shelf on the wall next to the cottage door, his welcoming smile the first thing she saw upon arrival. Surrounded by four mounted largemouth bass that different family members had caught in the lake, the picture showed her father, seated in his green bass-fishing boat, wrapped in a warm, woolen, handmade sweater, a grand smile beaming on his face. Amy's brother, Eric, had snapped the picture, taken in front of a dilapidated old boathouse in Morton's Creek, at one of her father's favorite Lake Beverly fishing spots. Year after year, Mr. Montgomery observed the decline of that particular boathouse by having a family member take a picture of him in front of it. In this picture, only a portion of the roof remained visible, her father's hands grasping the oars of his boat. He looked happy, but pale and withdrawn. It was the final photo taken in front of the boathouse. Amy wondered if the structure had survived over the years; her father hadn't.

Although Amy enjoyed visiting the cabin, each day brought a mixture of sadness and pain. She could not set foot inside the green bass boat that her father used whenever he fished; panic attacks overwhelmed her whenever she tried to get into the boat. Her heart pounded loudly, she became light-headed and nauseous, her body trembled, and she felt like she was about to jump out of her skin. She remained on the dock whenever James went out for a fishing trip. Most of the time, James Jr. stayed behind, too.

As the week of vacation drew to an end, sadness filled their hearts. James and Jim Jr. were always reluctant to leave the cabin, and Amy's grief for her father escalated, as they got ready to depart. The time came to pack the Honda and return to Pennsylvania. Safely secured in their seatbelts, they searched for their favorite radio station and rode quietly along the winding road to the border. Abbey, to their delight, was an excellent traveler. After ten minutes on the road, she'd head for the floor, curl up and nap. What a trooper!

As years passed, she realized how hard her father had worked to leave that legacy behind for his children. Every inch of the lakefront cabin held indescribable feelings of nostalgia and peace, and anyone who spent time at Lake Beverly, family member or friend, departed as though they had left a piece of their hearts behind. Amy vowed to instill that same love of the lake within her own family.

When they returned home, Amy's radiography diploma was waiting for her in the mail. She was so proud! She had prepared extensively for the two-hour test, and her grade was 94%. She'd known she'd done well, but holding the certificate made her feel a sense of self-satisfaction. She was intelligent enough—she had attended the classes, studied hard for the exam and earned a good grade. She felt competent and confident. The very next day, she began to take patients' oral radiographs. Eventually, she might be offered additional hours and an increase in salary. She'd contribute to her family's income—she had begun another stage in her career. She no longer had to feel the low self-esteem and self-worth she'd felt when she was "only" a homemaker and mother, as though those roles were something of which she should be ashamed. She was moving forward, toward something more, albeit slowly and carefully.

August rolled in. Although she was happier at home and work, her cigarette dependency still ruled her. She felt sick and enervated, noticing subtle changes in her body that worried her. She waited for her period to come, but because of her eating disorder, her menstrual cycles had always been erratic. Occasionally, she had a normal, 28-day cycle. More usually, she went 30 or 40 days between periods, sometimes skipping them altogether. Her low weight was responsible, as she had found out at the Windsor. Even though she didn't have a period, she had premenstrual symptoms, with cramps and nausea, and was more irritable. She knew she should quit smoking, but the cigarettes helped stabilize her daily anxiety. Just thinking about quitting made her nervous.

With the change in seasons, Amy was distracted, worried about the beginning of the new school year and stressed about paying end-of-the-year insurance bills and property taxes. When she approached the 40-day mark without her period, she panicked and bought a home pregnancy test at the drugstore downtown. The following morning, August 12, she collected a urine sample and performed the test. To her surprise, the test was positive—she was pregnant! This was not supposed to happen, not now. How could she carry and nurture her unborn child, when she struggled to take care of herself? She must do everything in her power to help the baby survive.

She broke the news to James that evening. They were both frightened. Amy tried to remain calm and in control of her emotions. She prayed to God to grant her the strength she needed. Nutrition came first. She replaced coffee with fruit juices and milk. Although she felt so guilty about the cigarettes, she couldn't quit. How could she quit? She'd spend the whole day in a state of anxiety and panic, which would not be good for the baby. She did cut down considerably, but each time she experienced discomfort or cramps, she blamed the smokes.

She made an appointment with her obstetrician, anxiously awaiting the day of her visit. Amy relayed the news to her mother, who seemed very happy for them. James's mother, Nanny, was thrilled to have another grandchild on the way.

Amy's first trimester was unsettling, as it is for most women. Her emotional state spiked and plummeted each day as the increase in hormones brought daily changes to her body and mind. She focused on eating more food, tried to quit smoking and became angry with herself for getting pregnant and her husband for getting her pregnant. She was worried about her job, how she would continue to take radiographs if she was pregnant. The atmosphere in their home was turbulent.

The day of the big appointment arrived, and the doctor confirmed that Amy was pregnant. At 35 years of age, Amy had a greater risk of experiencing complications during pregnancy and having a child with a congenital anomaly, such as Down's syndrome. She immediately began to worry about having a miscarriage. The doctor suggested that Amy have an amniocentesis, which could be performed as an outpatient at Hershey Medical Center, in Hershey, Pennsylvania. A procedure in which a small amount of amniotic fluid is withdrawn from the uterus, an amniocentesis would test for birth defects and other potential problems. It was a minor procedure that only took about 15 minutes, but Amy could only get it done after her 15th week of pregnancy. The doctor would inject a local anesthetic into Amy's abdomen, and then insert a needle to withdraw a sample of amniotic fluid. A lab technician would culture the cells and have the results within three to four weeks. In addition to showing any potential congenital problems, the amniocentesis would also reveal the gender of the child.

After she and James discussed the procedure, they agreed it was best to do the amniocenteses. If, indeed, there were a problem with the baby, they'd know about it before the child was born, so they could prepare themselves for the worst. It would be several weeks before the baby was far along enough for Amy to get the procedure; until then, she would pray every day for a healthy baby. Amy believed God must have granted her another chance to live, and even if the baby weren't completely perfect, she and James would love it, nonetheless. The child was a gift, as was their first-born and her husband; three reasons for her to live.

Amy's split personality—angel vs. demon—was again battling for control over her. The demon welcomed and encouraged her guilt about her low calorie intake, her smoking and her fears about her career. She had to tell her employers about her condition; the dental x-rays were unsafe for the fetus. Could she take a maternity leave with this child? Would she be able to find good, affordable childcare and return to work? Should she go through with the amniocentesis? She felt like she had been shattered into a million pieces; she didn't have the first clue about how to become whole again. Dr. Lora had said one child was enough for Amy, but there she was, recovering from anorexia and conceiving another child. What was wrong with her? Distressed and depressed, she vented her anger at James. After all she had put him through, would he ever forgive her?

Her confessions in her daily journal were self-demeaning and degrading, more evidence of the demon within her. She was worried about the Prozac; without it, she felt chaotic and disoriented. She needed the antidepressant to correct her body's chemical imbalance. She was glad she'd stopped taking it—who knew how it would have affected her baby, had she still been taking Prozac when she'd conceived—but what would have happened if she had continued to take it? Would inner torment have subsided? Her continued depressive state was not her fault! She had inherited the tendency toward depression from someone genetically close, and yet emotionally distant from her. Amy refused to live her life like her mother had, and yet she was constantly pulled in that direction—downward, further into depression. Did she have the will—or the power—to let the angel within her take over?

In September, Jim entered second grade. At that time, her journal reflected a positive state of mind. Her first trimester—and worries about a miscarriage—was behind her. On September 16, she heard the baby's heartbeat for the first time. She felt an excited glow within her body. It was time to tell little Jim and the rest of her family the good news. The angel told her to take care of herself and the baby, to feel the child within her womb and watch her abdomen grow with life. The angel said, "You can do this, Amy."

When they told him about the baby, Jim Jr. was excited and inquisitive, wanting to know when the baby would be born and whether he would have a brother or a sister. Nanny was skeptical, telling Amy frankly to stop smoking and to eat more. Although she knew her mother-in-law was trying to help, Amy needed some distance after that conversation; she loved James's mother, but she could be very demanding. Amy's sister-in-law was also skeptical saying, "Well, you'll have to eat now, won't you?" Yes, she would. Amy had hoped for more support, but it was clear that the family had lost faith in her—she had certainly given them enough reason.

Before the amniocentesis, which was scheduled for October 20, Amy researched more about the procedure; she wanted to prepare herself. If the test results were positive, she knew she could endure the rest of the pregnancy. She had matured; she had experience in the role of motherhood. She'd do what felt right for herself and her family. If the results were negative, well, they'd cross that bridge when they came to it.

In therapy, Amy had learned to take one day at a time. Why worry about the next week, month or year, when she had no control over future events? Worrying about such things was not logical. She was very hard on herself, searching out problems, creating disruptions, simply to have something over which to worry. She loved misery and doom. Had her mother taught Amy that, too?

On the day of the procedure, young Jim went off to school, as usual, and then Amy and her husband drove to the Hershey Medical Center, where they spent a good part of the day. Later, Amy wondered how she had ever gotten through the experience, which wasn't painful, but rather harrowing. After all the preparation, the routine procedure was completed quickly and successfully, and they were on the road home by early afternoon. Amy had been instructed to perform only light duties at home and work and warned that she could possibly experience minor discomfort and cramping. The test results would arrive within three weeks; the hospital mailed the results on a blue or pink postcard, with the color of the card indicating the gender of the child. The waiting period began. Amy didn't know how she was going to survive three weeks!

She was thankful her job and husband kept her mind occupied. James was strong and levelheaded, mature and wise, forgiving, supportive, tolerant and endlessly patient. Amy could have filled dozens of journal pages with writing about his wit and wisdom, his stance and direction, his green, Irish eyes and crooked smile, his left-handed disposition and his unique personality. He was a likable, lovable man, and she thanked God every day for bringing him into her life.

Their faith in God and prayer was powerful. Amy prayed daily for strength, relaxing with deep-breathing exercises and handing her fears to God. "Help me, dear Lord," she prayed, "Take my hand. I believe in You, I believe in myself." She felt the strength He gave her. She would survive.

As the days passed, Amy began to feel the flutter of movement within her womb. She remembered the sensation when she carried her firstborn, James. Every few days, she felt the new life growing within her. What an extraordinary feeling!

She consumed three meals a day; however, she wasn't able to incorporate a wide variety of foods into her diet. Her cigarette dependency cut back to only five or six a day; extreme guilt overcame her each time she lit one up. She remembered the experience of withdrawal when she had previously quit smoking; she could not add that stress to her mind right now.

Her belly began to expand. Now that her pregnancy was physically obvious, she was becoming uneasy. She decided against purchasing maternity clothing, which she would only wear for a few months, and instead purchased larger-sized women's clothing. Big clothes worked for her—not a problem at all! She'd still be hidden. As she knew, one of the classic symptoms of anorexia was hiding your body under oversized clothing. Even when she wasn't pregnant, her clothes were large and loose fitting on her tiny frame. Anorexia skewed her perceptions of herself, so that she thought she appeared larger than she actually was; her clothing was always a size too big, purchased large because she really thought she was that size.

Two weeks before the results were due, Amy began to fantasize that a pink postcard would arrive in the mailbox. If she had a girl, she would have the "perfect family": one son and one daughter. She daydreamed about a tiny, blonde, blue-eyed baby girl, someone who would play with dolls and jump ropes, dresses and braids, sugar and spice, and everything nice. Ah, Amy's perfect world again!

On November 8, the Hershey Medical Center postcard arrived in the mail. It was blue. "From the Division of Genetics, The Milton S. Hershey Medical Center," it read. "We have completed the chromosomal analysis on the fetal cells obtained from your amniocentesis procedure. The results of our study show a normal male chromosomal pattern in the fetus. Please keep in mind that these results do not guarantee a 'normal' baby." If there were any questions, they could contact the Medical Center or her physician.

Amy's initial reaction was disappointment: her little-girl dreams came to an abrupt halt. She feared she would feel outnumbered by the opposite sex. Then she thought about their pet lhasa apsos, Abbey, who was female. She was certainly a part of their family, too! She was Amy's girl. This baby would be another son for James and her and a brother for Jim Jr. Their prayers had been heard and answered. A normal chromosomal pattern meant the child was healthy in that respect. If she wanted him to be as healthy as possible, Amy had to nurture him as well as herself for the remainder of the gestation period.

In January, Amy celebrated her 35th birthday. Blissless for her, birthdays usually left her feeling depressed. She never deserved—or was worthy of—a compliment of any kind, so why should anyone wish her a "Happy Birthday?" James bought her fresh flowers every year. He knew how she loved them and never turned them away, no matter how worthless she felt. As Amy carefully cut each long stem and arranged them perfectly in her crystal-cut vase, the green vine and ivy placed delicately behind the floral grouping, she felt her dark mood lift. She hummed as she baked her birthday cake, which everyone would enjoy. On this birthday, she had a slice for herself, which set her mind into a spin. It had taken her years to accept her own birthday as a special day—she had wasted so much precious time.

After her birthday, Amy's mood swings returned. She was fatigued, cranky and worried, and she wondered if she'd carry the baby to full term. Her hormones were in a frenzy. She had appointments with her gynecologist every three weeks, and then two weeks, and then every week. The doctor said she was due on April 11. Although she gained weight moderately into the third trimester, Amy concealed her pregnancy well, carrying the little one very low in her uterus, his position all up front. They needed to ready the baby's nursery—the spare bedroom was wallpapered in a floral motif, not at all appropriate for a baby boy. Amy's sister-in-law had a talent for wallpaper and borders, so Jim and Amy asked for her help. They chose a simple, striped pattern; out went the spare bed, and in came the crib, a changing table, tiny infant outfits and the marvelous, melt-your-heart "baby aroma," the scent of baby lotion and powder, and delicate detergent and shampoo. She and James felt love within that room, a sense of creation and new life.

It was time to name this young lad. Naturally, Amy purchased the ultimate baby-name book, and she and James poured over it together. She had her heart set on John, after her father, but James wanted Aloysius, after his own father. They both agreed that Mr. Bailey's name was a bit unusual, and so as to be fair to both of them, they decided to name their new son after neither of their fathers: Their son's name would be Shawn. It was an Irish name, for his heritage, and translated from Irish, Shawn meant "John." The name was perfect.

As her due date drew near, her nights became sleepless and restless nights. She'd awaken at night with her entire body trembling and shivering in a cold sweat. She didn't know if she was experiencing normal, pregnancy-related symptoms, or if she was just filled with tremendous guilt and worry. She tried to focus on positive thoughts. When she became over-tired and irritable, she sat down to take a break, relinquishing, for the few months of her pregnancy, the idea that everything had to be in its proper place. She focused on chores and tasks that were most important.

With six weeks to go, she had two weeks left to work before her maternity leave. Were they ready? Would she and James become close again? They seemed distant and separated. They needed time together, but they wouldn't have it for a long time.

March came in like a lion, indeed! A few days before St. Patrick's Day, a major snowstorm hit, named the "Blizzard of '93." Nanny traditionally prepared a grand, Irish celebration for the Saturday closest to the St. Patrick's Day, but that year, no one made it to her house for the party: The snow was over 24 inches deep!. Jim and Amy could not get outdoors. Jim had to shovel his way out of their basement door, and the schools were all closed for the entire week. Amy tried to shake off the feelings of restlessness that bothered her during that week. It was the end of winter, and most people in the Northeast had cabin fever. It was cold and snowy—it was supposed to be!

As her time grew near, she began making last-minute changes to the baby's room. On March 23, young Jim was 8 years old and preparing for the Sacraments of Reconciliation and his First Holy Communion, usually held in the months of March and May, respectively. These were two of the seven sacraments celebrated in the Catholic Faith. In May, Jim's new brother could be present for the ceremonial mass. That evening, Amy lay in bed, exhausted after the day's excitement. She felt some slight cramping and a few mild contractions, but thought little of it. Then, unexpectedly, her water broke. The time had come. Shawn had decided to enter the world a few weeks early.

Welcome, Shawn

James awoke his son, helped Amy into the car and drove to Nanny's house. She awaited their arrival from the porch, hurrying her grandson inside as his parents drove to the hospital.

They were excited and anxious parents-to-be. One week had passed since the blizzard, and a new storm front was approaching, heralded by sleet and freezing rain, which made the drive a bit more hazardous. They both sighed with relief when they finally arrived at the hospital. After admission, they were taken to the maternity floor. The head nurse wheeled Amy to the birthing room and alerted her obstetrician. Between contractions, Amy rested and held James's hand. In those serene moments, she prayed for Shawn's delivery to be quick and smooth. At one point, a nurse entered the room to relay a message to Amy. Her sister, Susan, in California, had called the hospital to send Amy good wishes. Susan said that Amy was in her thoughts and that she loved her. Amy began to cry; Susan's support meant so much to her.

Her labor with James had been short, only three-and-a-half hours. With this second baby, it was even less: two hours. Shawn arrived at 1:23 a.m. on March 24, 1993. He weighed only 6 pounds, which Amy attributed to the few cigarettes she smoked each day, as well as her nutritional deficiencies. Amy had gained 14 pounds with this pregnancy, as opposed to 20 with her first. God carried her all the way.

Amy held Shawn tenderly in her arms, as did his father. They called their mothers next, and James stayed by her side until morning, when he went home to rest and drive young Jim from Nanny's to school. In two days, all four of them came home. Young Jim's celebration of First Penance was that upcoming Saturday morning; thankfully, Shawn slept peacefully throughout the church service. He was four days old.

Amy soon found out that there was much more to do when there were two children! James helped quite a bit, but Amy felt exhausted all the time. Amy had a six-month maternity leave from the dental office. She wanted to continue to work, if she could make childcare arrangements with which she and James were comfortable. If she had to decide right then, she would have said there was no way she could have an infant, an 8 year old, and a job. Fortunately, she had until mid-September to decide. Even though they were exhausting, Amy would not have given up Shawn or James for anything in the world. Her two handsome young lads kept her in the land of the living.

During her maternity leave, Amy had difficulty dealing with her mother-in-law. Although Nan was a wonderful person, wife and mother, she had this overpowering disposition and could be so persistent and demanding. Generally, it was Nan's way, or no way! Having a timid personality, Amy never voiced her own opinion or opposition to Nan. Instead, she internalized her response to Nan's demands, requests and decisiveness, becoming angry and resentful toward her mother-in-law. Nan followed old wives tales and traditions that, to Amy, seemed outdated, untruthful and quite unbelievable at times. "Hashki," Nanny called them as youngsters, an old Irish word for "little one." Amy knew she meant well, but Nan made her feel as though she was not doing a very good job at mothering, as she had done with Jim. This made Amy exceedingly uncomfortable whenever they visited her, and many times they avoided her altogether.

With her second-born child, the nurturing and bonding experiences were less stressful. She had experience this time around—she did not need to follow any textbooks! Wherever she took young James, she wrapped Shawn and settled him in his booster car seat, and off they went. They traveled to and from school, to Sunday masses, to Jim's First Holy Communion, his minor league baseball games, Saturday-morning bowling league and a family reunion that summer. They skipped their annual vacation to the lake that year; instead, they opted for daily trips to amusement parks and museums. It was a nice change, and Amy was learning, in small steps, that changes are beneficial. We all need change to thrive and grow, to endure life's challenges and pursue dreams.

As Shawn grew to six months of age, James and Amy decided that they didn't feel comfortable entrusting their son to a day-care center, even one near her office. She told Dr. Anthony that she could not return to work at that time. She was disappointed—she had made tremendous progress at the dental practice—however, it was more important to be home with the children.

Throughout her pregnancy, Amy's nicotine dependency diminished. When September came, she kicked the repulsive habit for good. Around the same time, she began to write in her journal again. Her angel resurfaced from time to time; the demon kept her subdued. Her journal entries remained overwhelmingly negative and because she was no longer eating for two, her eating disorder resurfaced. She cut her hair; this time it was "boy" short. Amy called it "no fuss," but she knew she needed to be less visible. She was rigid and unsatisfied. She felt no enjoyment for anything. She had no purpose.

During this time, young Jim continued to have the night frights. In addition to his response to his mother's illness and depression, he was learning to cope with the arrival of a sibling. James Jr. had had the rule of the house for eight years. He had to learn to share love and attention with his brother.

When the boys became ill with colds or the flu, Amy could not think rationally. Her nerves went haywire! The vomiting phobia she had developed as a child had carried into her adulthood. Her mind was set on this path of perfection, and she had no tools for coping with these daily situations, imperfect and faulty. She felt petrified every day and night; terrified the boys would become ill. She was constantly in a state of panic.

Three years had passed since she had been hospitalized in

Philadelphia. In January of 1994, she received a letter from the Graduate Hospital Eating Disorder Unit, informing her that the Windsor Unit was closed. She was saddened, thinking back to that time and the women she had met, and she wondered where women with eating disorders would go now. She thought about the Prozac, wondering if she should resume taking it now that her pregnancy was over. Her mind and body were in such turmoil, but with two children and one income, they could never afford it. The drug was too expensive. She could live without it.

That winter, the boys came down with stomach viruses and flu that made them nauseous and under the weather for two weeks straight. After that, they contracted the chicken pox. Although she'd been warned of them for years, it wasn't until now that Amy experienced her first panic attack. She couldn't breathe, and her heart throbbed. She began to sweat, feel weak and hyperventilate. She felt as though she would lose consciousness—and all because she had a phobia about sickness and vomiting. These were her children! What had she become? After her sons were better, Amy fell further into depression, hitting a low she'd never before experienced. It was then that she declared she would live to age 45; she couldn't imagine her body existing for any longer. It would shut down, and she'd perish.

By summertime, she was noticeably thinner. In her journal, she wrote that she resembled a zombie. When fall came, thoughts of suicide returned, and she knew she was in trouble. She felt gray, numb and in limbo; she was drowning. Even as she watched her own self decline, she noticed that her mother was becoming even frailer. Amy feared her mother's death, realizing it might be imminent.

In November, she gathered the strength to attend a seminar on depression held at her local hospital. Comprised of a small group of men and women, the seminar featured a video that explained the signs and symptoms of depressive illness, with a discussion afterward, a question-and-answer session and an opportunity for evaluation. Each participant filled out a questionnaire; Amy was surprised (or was she, really?) by the number of questions to which she answered "yes": low energy, feeling overwhelmed by the smallest challenges, sleep disturbances, difficulty in experiencing joy, feelings of guilt and worthlessness and thoughts of suicide. That night, she discussed the seminar with James. She wanted to see her family physician and get the help she needed. In December, she began to take Zoloft, a new antidepressant her doctor prescribed. She prayed to God it would help her.

After two months, the Zoloft still was not effective. Amy's doctor put her back on Prozac, the antidepressant she had taken in the past. Although James assured her the expense was worth the benefits, Amy felt incredibly guilty for needing the medication. James promised they could manage. She had to take the medication for four to six weeks before she would notice any concrete changes in her mental stability. She waited and prayed.

Throughout the summer months, young Jim played Little League baseball, while James, Amy and Shawn watched from the sidelines. As they rooted for Jim, they also pitched balls and played catch with Shawn. He was a major follower of his brother's sporting events and always had a ball in his hands.

In Shawn's toddler years, Amy tried to become more involved in programs especially for young children. She joined her Public Library Toddler Reading Program, held once a week. She enrolled him in swimming lessons at the YMCA, as well as a movement class with hands-on activities. She tried to keep active, rather than secluded. She did not want to impose the same fears on Shawn as she had on young Jim.

She allowed her hair to grow again, and when Jim told her how attractive she looked, she almost believed him. On their vacation at the lake in the summer of 1995—Amy's sister, Ann, and her family joined them—she had a major breakthrough. She wasn't certain what caused it, whether it was the Prozac or some change within herself, but she was finally able to get into her father's boat. Amy, James, her sons and their dog, Abbey, spent an afternoon on the lake, fishing and watching the waterfowl. Somehow, she had overcome the panic and anxiety she had stored inside her for eight years, since her father died. She was so proud of herself that day!

James Jr. entered the sixth grade, and Shawn would enter preschool the following year. James suggested a wonderful employment opportunity—he asked Amy if she had ever considered working as a teacher's aide in their children's school district. Her experience with office work and her CPR certification would certainly qualify her. James reminded her that school days would be work days, and when the kids were out of school, Amy would be off from work. What could be better than that? She'd work the days and hours Shawn was in preschool and be back in time for James to arrive home from school. Amy loved the idea! She immediately contacted the district's administrative office and requested the necessary forms. After she completed, signed and returned them, she had to wait for the forms to be processed, and then she would be placed on the call list as a substitute aide.

As Amy was pursuing a new career, her mother once again considered retiring from the bank. Computer technology had made its way into the finance industry, and each bank branch sent its tellers to computer-based training. These changes made Mrs. Montgomery uncomfortable; with failing health and at her age in life, the idea of learning to use a computer overwhelmed her. She was ready to step aside and offer the opportunity to a younger, more ambitious individual. Within six month, she retired.

After her retirement, Amy's mother took two very important, positive steps forward. She realized that her health would have only suffered further from the additional stress if she had continued to keep working, and she decided she needed to relax more. The second change, for which Amy was most thankful, was her mother's acceptance of her family physician's diagnosis of depression. She began taking Zoloft. Since Amy first found out about antidepressants, she had known her mother would benefit from them, even more so after her mother became a widow. Within two months, the changes were remarkable. Mrs. Montgomery wasn't as negative and had fewer complaints. She no longer let her feelings about her health, friends and family—even her daily existence—drag her down. Amy actually began to feel comfortable when she visited her mother, no longer filled with anxiety and pain. Because her mother was no longer sinking further into depression, she ceased to pull Amy down with her.

When Thanksgiving approached, her mother and Amy's youngest brother, Joseph, still at home, went out for dinner instead of cooking a meal she dreaded. Finally, Mrs. Montgomery realized that she did not have to cook a huge turkey with all the trimmings. She took the stress off of herself, and then did something she wanted to do: ate a nice dinner she hadn't had to make. As if that weren't change enough, at Christmastime, she purchased gifts by catalog instead of miserably shopping in the mall or asking Amy to do the shopping for her. Every year, Amy had to shop for at least a few gifts her mother wanted to give, and then wrap everything for her mother. Because Amy had to do everything perfectly, wrapping presents was a chore that brought her a great deal of anxiety and stress. She did keep to the tradition of Christmas Eve, though, but that year, she asked everyone to take part in the preparations, relieving herself of her usual stress. Everyone had a great time that year, even Amy.

Amy and her mother talked about Amy's potential job with the school district. Mrs. Montgomery told her daughter that she'd help her out with Shawn in any way that she could, including baby-sitting. Since her mother had never offered to baby-sit for either of Amy's children, she was especially happy with this change in her mother's attitude. For the first time, Amy felt her mother was honestly concerned about her. She wanted Amy to live her own life. She wanted to help Amy open her eyes to life, to help her move away from the path she'd been set upon since childhood. Only one thing made Amy sad: Her mother had waited so long to get help—she was in her mid-60s by that time, after struggling with a lifetime of her depression. As had been the case with Amy's father, she only came to know her mother after she had retired. So much precious time had been wasted.

It seemed as though Amy had been waiting forever to begin work with the school district. The first call finally came one Sunday evening: The superintendent needed a substitute for an aide who worked with a learning-supported student. Teacher's aides worked with special education, learning and emotional support, and life skills students in the classroom. She might also be asked to work as a substitute office or building aide. The hours varied from four-and-a-half to six-and-a-half daily, depending upon which of the district's ten schools she was asked to work at on a given day. Amy would accept calls from any school that requested an aide for that particular workday.

She called her mother that Sunday evening and told her the good news. In preparation for when Amy would work, she or James took Shawn to her mother's house in the morning, or sometimes she came up to their house to watch him. The arrangement was working well; Mrs. Montgomery soon became familiar with her grandson's favorite television shows and regular activities. He was an active and mobile child, who loved sports and who was always in motion. Nana pitched baseballs to him in the backyard. Soon, when he began to hit them out of the yard, she'd walk up the block or into the alley to retrieve them. One day, she told Amy that she hoped she would be able to see Shawn play Little League baseball, as she had with James Jr. Amy was thrilled at the interest her mother was taking in her grandchildren's lives.

As a substitute aide, each day was a new and challenging experience; she never knew where she'd be called to work, or in what setting, until she arrived at the school. Amy loved working at the various schools—everything about the job was rewarding, especially her interactions with the children. These special kids opened her eyes, her heart and her mind, bringing to the surface a part of her she had never known existed. She guided and supported them—physically, visually and educationally—throughout their school days. Although she had been worried that she wouldn't know what to do, she soon found there weren't any right or wrong ways to do things, just the best way she knew how, learned from her years of experience raising her own two children. Finally, for the first time, she realized she had a special quality: She was really good at working with children. She nurtured this talent, wishing she had more educational training, professional guidance and the techniques the regular teachers had learned. She had so much to discuss when she came home; every day was different. There were so many different children, with so many different needs. She began to understand that the people in her life- James, Jim and Shawn- were so very, very precious.

Whenever a permanent, part-time position was posted in the school offices, she applied. Eventually, as she gained more seniority, she'd get hired as an aide. Her day would come. Until then, she would continue to enjoy working with the different children she encountered each day. For the first time, she felt alive. She finally had a purpose.

Amy's Mother

One year had passed since Amy began working, and she noticed a substantial lapse in her journal writings. Since she only wrote when she was feeling anxious or upset, Amy considered taking herself off the Prozac. She felt better, and she still felt guilty for the amount of money the antidepressants cost her family each month. They could certainly use the money for other bills. Gradually, without her physician's knowledge, she weaned herself from the drug.

On July 15, 1997, she wrote in her journal that she no longer wanted to be dependent on any antidepressants, writing: *If her heart should give, she'd leave all the love inside it to her sons. They could carry it with them, for they'd know how deeply she loved them and how little she loved herself...* Although she could not see it at the time, she later realized that the sequence of events corresponding with her time on Prozac formed an obvious pattern: When Amy was taking the antidepressants, she felt stable and less distressed. When she stopped, she plummeted, the two sides of her personality constantly tormenting each other. How she wished, later in life, that she had realized what she was doing when she stopped taking the Prozac!

On a serene morning that summer, Amy sat at her kitchen table and wrote, searching intently for another piece of the puzzle. She felt a heavy weight in her heart. She wrote about the mid to late 1990s, about her mother, trying to prepare herself for what the future held. Her mother was taking more and more medication, frequently visiting different physicians for the vast number of ailments that plagued her. In the spring of 1997, she had lost her faithful canine companion, Spot. Her mother never shed a tear from the loss, but Amy saw how emotionally immobilized she became afterward. She was frailer, thinner, paler and smaller. Amy feared her death was near. As Amy prepared for that day, she began, once again, to keep close watch over the one aspect in her life that she could control: food. Without the Prozac, she became unstable and unbalanced. The bathroom scale was her haven, her glorious accomplishment—as long as the numbers stayed the same or decreased.

In September, Shawn started preschool, Jim entered junior high and Amy continued to substitute for the district. Amy's mother was hospitalized for a few days, for tests, the doctor said, but Amy worried, nonetheless. Working kept Amy focused; keeping house kept her hidden. The numbers on the scale dropped, one by one, 105, 103, 100 lbs..

November 8 of that year would have been Amy's parents' 50th wedding anniversary. Mrs. Montgomery wanted to plan a family gathering to celebrate the event, but Amy could not understand why her mother wanted a party. Her father had been gone for 10 years— how could they celebrate their Golden Anniversary? Aside from her feelings about her father, worried about how difficult the day would be, Amy's mind immediately associated "family dinner party" with "eating food in front of people." Knowing her family's eyes would be watching her, she already felt uncomfortable. Amy, of course, made all the arrangements for the affair, selecting a restaurant and handling all the other plans. She drove her mother to the restaurant one Saturday afternoon, and they sat with the events hostess and discussed the menu, date and time of the occasion. They telephoned the whole family to make sure everyone reserved that date in November on their calendars. Every one of the seven children, and their families, attended. Susan flew in from California, and John and his family stayed for the weekend. As the date drew near, Amy's anxiety grew exponentially.

Mrs. Montgomery, her children and her grandchildren numbered 21 that Sunday in November. They took numerous photographs of everyone there, including different shots of individual families, groups of siblings and grandchildren. Amy blocked the dinner out of her mind altogether. She managed to eat something, but she was extremely self-conscious throughout the meal. Amy did remember one of her siblings making a hurtful comment about their father at the dinner table, which was unsettling to her, but she couldn't recall exactly what was said.

When Amy looked at the pictures from that night, she saw how gaunt and ashen her mother appeared. She grinned without showing her teeth, and her posture was slightly bent over, as if she were holding in some great pain. She looked as if she might break. Amy, in the photos, had shoulder-length, slightly curly hair. She weighed less than 90 pounds, and her clothing hung from her bones. She had stopped menstruating again. She, too, looked as though she were in pain. Like mother, like daughter, it seemed.

In January, Amy reached a milestone: Much to her dismay, she turned 40—the same year the Barbie doll celebrated her 40th birthday of manufacture. Ironically, Amy never had a Barbie. Her girlfriends had them, she remembered, but Amy had a doll named "Tammy," larger than a Barbie and not as petite, pretty or slender. Amy kept that Tammy doll in perfect condition, tucking it away in its original case. She had also saved a Chatty Cathy doll and a doll named Drowsy; however, Cathy no longer chatted and Drowsy no longer cried when you pulled her arm down. Amy felt more like the worn, damaged Chatty Cathy and Drowsy dolls than she did the Tammy doll—let alone the glamorous Barbie. Nevertheless, on Amy's birthday, a package arrived from Amy's charming, cheerful sister-in-law. Carefully wrapped in delicate birthday paper was a Special Edition Arctic Barbie Doll, dressed in a fawn-colored, fur-trimmed outfit, with matching fur-tipped suede boots. Amy was elated! At age 40, she had received her first Barbie.

The boys kept Jim and Amy active all winter long, with basketball games at the YMCA with Jim Jr. and a weekly bowling league with Shawn, who turned five in March; Jim became a teenager in June. When their elder son completed his Little League baseball career, the younger began his. The children continued to keep Amy vital. At Easter, Amy's aunt and uncle on her father's side came to visit from Sacramento with their youngest daughter. Jim and Amy had visited these relatives when they were on their honeymoon in 1979, and they always held a special place in Amy's heart. Amy and her aunt wrote to each other occasionally, and Amy always included pictures of the boys. Still, Amy flashed back to the last time they had come east to Pennsylvania; it was the summer before her father passed away. She felt restless.

After almost a year of silence, Amy was writing in her journal again. As Amy wrote down her thoughts and feelings, it helped her release the pain, anxiety and difficult emotions bottled up within her. From time to time, since her therapy years, she had written many letters and notes to the people in her life. In a kind and honest way, she might have written about an incident or a person that troubled her, a method for coping with difficult situations. She also enjoyed writing letters of support, encouragement and congratulations. She needed to release both kinds of feelings to others: positive and troublesome.

In addition to her journal writing, Amy worked overtime to keep her mind occupied. She worked part-time during the school year, but her summers were free. She decided to find a summer job, so she could better assist her family with finances. She applied for a cake-decorating job at their new Wal-Mart Super Center, a job she thought would be interesting, challenging and fun. She began in May of 1998, working four-to-five-hour shifts two or three days a week. Nanny usually watched the boys for an hour or so, until James came in from work. Amy also worked Sunday mornings, when Jim and the boys were still in bed.

Subconsciously, Amy was running away from the reality of the emotionally disturbing events that were happening: her mother's health was failing. Amy welcomed any amount of diversion. She went back to the short haircut again, just before they left for their Canada vacation. This year, they spent time with her brother, Matthew, and his daughter, Heather. It was the year of Beanie Babies, those adorable, bean-stuffed, gotta-have-'em animals; Heather had over 100 of them in her collection. James's sister and her husband rented a place on Bob's Lake, not far from Lake Beverly, and the families visited on both lakes throughout the week.

Mrs. Montgomery had not been to the lake for two years. She was uncomfortable making the lengthy drive and was afraid of having a health emergency in another country. Amy was nervous about leaving her mother behind that summer. She was not her usual self, and Amy sensed something was different. Her mother seemed a bit disoriented and lethargic. That summer the temperatures were intense, and her mother really struggled with the heat. Her appetite was poor and she appeared overly tired. She reassured her daughter that she was fine and insisted she go off to the cottage with her boys. Amy agreed, knowing her siblings were nearby and could tend to any problems her mother might have during Amy's vacation. She called her mother every day to check on her condition.

While at the lake that summer, Amy had a strong desire to visit and photograph landmarks: the Thousand Island Bridge, the Historical Building in a small fishing town called Delta, the Lyndhurst Bridge, which was hundreds of years old with a unique style and design, Wings Live Bait Store, where they annually purchased their fishing licenses, and souvenirs to remember their visit to the lake. Something was wrong. She felt sad, empty and alone. She tried desperately to find some sort of an answer for why she was so morose, but all she could come up with was that they should not have gone to Lake Beverly that year. She felt guilty for leaving her mother. When Amy called her mid-week, she sounded weak and short of breath. Ann prepared meals for her, and her brother, Eric, stopped to see her before work, but by the latter part of the week, she was hospitalized. Ann called and said their mother was dehydrated and weak and had experienced heart irregularities. Amy, Jim, Matthew and the children all came home immediately. Amy left a message for John and his family, who were on vacation in Cape May, and Susan, in Los Angeles, immediately checked flight availability for the trip home. Closer-to-home siblings were already aware of their mother's condition.

On the evening of their return from Canada, Amy and her family visited her mother in the hospital. She was being fed intravenously for her nutritional deterioration, and she needed a few days in the care of professionals, who could give her body a boost. The air-conditioned atmosphere was a relief to her after the extended heat wave. The nurses monitored her closely and regulated her medications. After a time, she rested comfortably.

Each day in the hospital brought additional health problems. Mrs. Montgomery. required oxygen for a breathing dysfunction. The doctors ordered numerous tests and x-rays of her heart and lungs. She contracted a slight case of pneumonia, and her appetite diminished further; at times, what she consumed, she regurgitated. Diagnosing diverticulosis, a condition in which the pouches of the colon become acutely inflamed, causing abdominal pain and fever, her physician requested a series of gastrointestinal tests, which revealed an obstruction in her bowel. Her abdomen enlarged, and the doctors performed emergency surgery.

Throughout all this, Amy had not heard from her brother, John. She called him again, finding that he had not received her message; an electrical storm had tripped his answering device. He flew in without delay; he and his wife taking time from their jobs. Susan arrived the next day, which was Friday.

The family waited, the air thick with tension, in a small waiting room, while their mother was in surgery. It was early Thursday evening. The hours seemed like days. Finally, the surgeon entered the room. He performed a colostomy, creating an artificial opening in the abdomen for elimination of body wastes, which, he explained, could be inadvertently reversed at a later time. Mrs. Montgomery had tolerated the procedure well and was in the recovery room, awaiting transfer to the ICU. Tests revealed she had experienced a mild myocardial infarction, or heart attack, but she was fine for the time being. The family members were allowed to visit her, one at a time, for a minute or so each. She was sedated and noticeably in pain. When everyone had seen her, they took the elevator to the first floor in silence. The family was numb.

By Friday morning, Amy's mother was having extreme difficulty breathing and consented to going on a ventilator. Amy heard this information from her brother, Eric, who had seen her early in the day. As soon as she heard her mother was on a ventilator, Amy lost all hope. When she saw her mother that afternoon, her soul emptied. Amy knew that her mother would not regain consciousness. Her fight would be over soon. It must have been horrible for Susan when she arrived late Friday afternoon. She was unable to speak to her mother, only gaze at her in that uncomfortable state.

Further complications developed over the weekend. Mrs. Montgomery had been on extensive antibiotic and nutritional intravenous tubes and had contracted an unidentified infection that was puzzling her doctors. Late Saturday afternoon, the family was informed that the hospital could no longer treat their mother's medical condition; they wanted to transfer her to Hahnamann Hospital in Philadelphia, where infectious disease specialists could better treat her. Life Flight helicopter flew Amy's mother to the Philadelphia facility.

Afterward, Amy vividly remembered waiting outside her mother's hospital room with her husband, brothers and sisters, while her mother was prepped for the transport. She was placed carefully on a stretcher and wheeled down the hallway, onto the elevator, and outside to the awaited helicopter. The family was instructed to stay inside the hospital until the medical helicopter took off. The sound of that copter would remain with Amy forever, as would the sight of it rising into the air, carrying her mother away from them. She prayed that the Philadelphia doctors could help her. Amy was frightened—they all were—but Amy was unreasonably upset because her mother was so far from home.

Mrs. Montgomery stayed two weeks at the Hahnneman Hospital. Amy later called the section of the hospital that her mother was in the "Next Step to Heaven" floor. The atmosphere was peaceful and serene; her mother appeared to be on a cloud. Fresh, crisp, white linens adorned her hospital bed, and her arms were carefully wrapped in soft, cottony gauze. Her bed was hydraulic, to keep her quiet, still body in gentle motion, ever so slowly. Amy later remembered the sounds of monitors and high-technology life-support equipment and machines, the machines that kept her mother alive.

Amy could never have prepared herself for the way she found her mother, that next day, when her brother Eric and his wife drove down and saw her. Amy's sister, Susan, guided her into the room. When Amy first saw her mother, her heart raced and she felt faint. Susan explained the monitors to Amy, the doctors, nurses and hospital staff, who all took such wonderful care of their mother. She was alive, and Amy heard the hope of recovery in Susan's voice. Amy saw a woman who was retaining a terrifying amount of fluid, lying in an obscure state of limbo. She recognized her mother, but knew she was gone. The next step for her was into the Kingdom of Heaven.

Their mother's loving heart held strong for two weeks. Horrified by the idea that her mother was in pain, Amy prayed to God every day to take her mother with Him. On August 22, 1998, at 3:00 A.M., Susan called from the hospital to say their mother was gone. Amy was downstairs in her rocker, with rosary beads in her hands, praying for God to care for her mother's soul.

All seven of Amy's family siblings gathered that afternoon to discuss the necessary arrangements for their mother and to read her last will and testament. Ann, the eldest, was the executor of the will. Amy had drawn her mother's important legal documents from her safe-deposit box at the bank back in November, before the dinner party. Amy had asked her mother when she wanted the papers returned to the bank for safekeeping, but her mother told her not to worry about them or bother having them secured. She obviously wanted her documents inside her home. She knew Amy would have access to them when she needed them.

Ann read the will to all of her siblings. She was responsible for taking care of the legal matters, payment of debts and funeral expenses. Their mother had done what she thought was best for all of her children. They accepted and respected her decisions.

When a loved one is lost, the feelings of sorrow and grief are indescribable. Death is very personal; it is very individual. For anyone who has experienced death, it is an understandable uniting of our human existence.

Life Goes On

Less than two weeks remained until Shawn entered kindergarten. Just as she remembered young Jim's first day, she sent Shawn off to be a big boy; dressed in new clothes, sneakers and backpack, he was all smiles and ready to go. Amy drove him to and from school.

Amy was overcome with grief. Many times, if she was not called out to substitute, she came home and crawled back into bed. Some days, she took the telephone receiver off the hook, shutting out the entire world. Although her mind felt dead and numb, her mind and body, amazingly, went on. She knew she was about to plunge into a deeper state of depression. She was unable to speak of what her family had been through, and she feared what lay ahead. She weighed 85 pounds. She was losing the battle.

After his first few weeks of school, Shawn suffered "kindergarten distress" and "school phobia." Unlike Jim, who had run out of the school after his mother, Shawn refused to get out of bed and get dressed in the morning. Amy was having a troublesome time with him. Using the bit of functional mind she had left, she called the school guidance counselor and met with him. He then spoke with Shawn, reassuring him that kindergarten was an adjustment for all children and everything would fall into place. He spoke with her son for a time, and then he returned to his class. Amy had asked for help, and she received it. She had almost forgotten what that was like.

She exited the school grounds and drove to the cemetery, sitting by her mother and father's gravesite, feeling overwhelming remorse. After a few minutes, she managed to drive home. As she pulled into her garage, she severely broke down, becoming confused, disoriented and shaky. Her legs wobbling, she walked across the street to her church's office and rectory. She clung to the doorway and told one of the staff that she needed help. Jean carefully took Amy by the arm and led her to Father Ed, who sat Amy down, held her hands and comforted her until the shaking subsided. He called James to come to the rectory and take her home. Amy was so empty and depleted. She never wanted to feel that dysfunctional again.

In a few weeks, Shawn had adjusted to his daily school routine, and Amy decided to cut back her cake-decorating hours at Wal-Mart. Substituting in the schools were more important. She worked at the bakery on Friday evenings and Sunday mornings only, enjoying the intricate, decorative styles, airbrushing the icing, creating leaves and flowers and writing the customers' wishes on the cakes. Fridays meant pick-up from school, home to change into her "whites," drop the boys at Nanny's, and then over to the bakery. She had to move constantly; she did not want free time, time alone to stop, dwell, think or feel. She feared the devastation and heartache she had felt that day with Father Ed.

The school district called more frequently, a situation that kept Amy focused on the children. That fall of 1998, she got to spend a few weeks at Shawn's school. She became more familiar with the students and staff there, which helped to keep her thoughts away from her mother.

"First" holidays and special occasions without her mother had begun: November 8, her parent's anniversary, Thanksgiving and Christmas. Amy evaded these occasions by working at the bakery. She had two part-time jobs that kept her on the run. The bakery involved hours of standing, walking and heavy lifting. She transported five-gallon tubs of icing and boxes of frozen cakes, cleaning up at her shift's end, and then mopping the floor. The few hours that she worked allowed only one short break, little time to get something to eat. Eighty-five pounds dropped to 83.

Unbeknownst to Amy, her family's time together in the hospital made them aware of her deteriorating condition. Her sister made a few phone calls, finding qualified people who could help. Amy did not follow through on any treatment at that time; she could not wrap her mind around her need for professional help. She had difficulty sleeping at night; whatever position she lay in, her hips, ribs and spine became numb, and she was often lightheaded, dizzy and weak. She was ashamed of how she must look to others: Her clothing hung on her, and she knew she was a frightening and ugly sight to everyone. She found it difficult to move on. Should she have called her doctor?

She was too embarrassed to ask. Life was passing her by. How could she end the damnation, the annihilation, and live again? She and James existed together, and yet were so very distant from one another.

The New Year brought brighter days. In January of 1999, an office secretary at her local school went on sick leave for six weeks. Amy was called to substitute for the position. She was elated! The school office was very busy and quite a challenge at times. It was very comfortable and convenient that she, Jim and Shawn could be in the same building. Amy understood the position was temporary and continued to apply for a permanent location. During that six-week period, an aide position was posted for the same school as her children. It was for an aide to work with kindergarten through third-grade learning-support students, a position with which Amy was already experienced. She immediately wrote a letter of interest to bid on the opening, taking it personally to the administrative office. It was her time.

In early February, she was notified that she had gotten the job. She was so happy! As soon as the aide returned from her leave into the office, Amy began in the classroom. She thanked God and her mother. They had a strategic plan for her, she believed. A permanent, part-time job in the same school as her children—what more could she want?

Looking back, Amy should have known that whenever something good happened to her, she began to break down inside. Her brainwaves seemed to reject happiness, instead pursuing disappointment and dejection. Her final journal entry was dated 4-21-99. She prayed to God, to take her fears and to help her to become strong. "Sleep, please let me sleep", she wrote.

Amy learned many new names the remainder of that school year, attached to many new faces. The children were an inspiration to her. Each child was unique, each child eager to learn at different paces. They all seemed to admire their teacher, looking to Amy for guidance and reassurance. She felt comfortable and blended well with the students, faculty and staff. Because a full-time position meant health, vision, dental and prescription-drug benefits for her and her family, she hoped that someday the position could become full-time. She had a goal in her mind.

That summer, Amy's entire family held a reunion at the cottage, renting another place nearby to accommodate everyone. Siblings, cousins and in-laws spent much-needed time together for one week. They wanted to stay connected. They held a fishing contest, had evening fireworks, reminisced and played with their children as they had as children themselves, on the land by the lake. The other siblings reminisced about their departed parents, but Amy could not speak much about her father, let alone her mother. It was all inside, stored away for safekeeping.

In mid July, Amy's mother-in-law, Nanny, celebrated her 80th birthday. She made it a very special occasion at a restaurant in town and invited all her family and closest friends, who showered her with gifts and a tremendous birthday cake. In Amy's eyes, it was a familiar setting: everyone gathered for the festive event, with Nanny appearing feeble and pale, just as had Amy's mother on her 50th anniversary party. Nan rarely visited the doctor, only taking one medication, for hypertension. Nevertheless, Amy knew she would be gone soon, just like her own mother.

God reached out to Mrs. Bailey on February 8, 2000: She grasped His hand and followed Him. Amy gathered with Jim's family. Whenever his family drifted apart, they called or got together; they united, for they loved one another. Amy was blessed in that her children felt the love their grandmothers had shared with them. Young James had so little time with his grandfathers, and Shawn did not have the chance to meet them at all.

Amy had survived. She'd made it through the most difficult of times. One by one, their parents' times had come, their places and purposes on the earth completed. A generation had passed, and the next was stepping up. A sense of peacefulness surrounded Amy and James, tranquility, silence and calmness. What mattered most in their lives was their family. They were blessed and gifted, and in return they were kind, generous and helpful to others. It made the world a better place.

Although Amy felt an external sense of peace, she experienced emptiness inside. As the heart is comprised of four chambers, each chamber, with each passing parent, became empty. Amy found comfort in her children, of course: How proud she was of her sons, with their accomplishments and achievements, overcoming their obstacles and struggles. Handsome and well mannered, they were respected, determined and gifted in many ways. They filled a section of Amy's heart with peace. Her husband, James, was her forever soul mate, strong and lighthearted, perseverant and proud, sensible, practical and witty. He was her love and passion and was always by her side, another chamber of her heart. The remainder of her heart continued to fill with all of the schoolchildren with whom she had contact. She taught each child that he or she was a very special person, no matter what his or her ability. Each one touched Amy, making a distinct impression within her. Her heart was endless in depth. Until her last day on earth, there would be room to spare. The pieces of her life slowly began to come together.

Schoolchildren

Kids, hundreds of exceptional kids, had become and integral part of Amy's everyday life. She had agreed to find part-time employment as a condition to her release from the Windsor, but she had never expected she would also find another purpose in life. She was motivated. She wanted to obtain as much knowledge as she could from the children's regular teachers; she listened intently, followed their techniques and tried to adopt their professional standards. She was eager to learn, realizing she had finally discovered what she wanted to do when she grew up: be a teacher. Better late than never! She had no desire to go to school for teaching credentials; being a teacher's aide suited her just fine. What better way to learn the ideals of education than to spend time each day in the classroom, watching professionals teach their students?

Children were certainly innocent and ingenuous. In the kindergarten class in Amy's second year, there were two sets of twins, identical girls and fraternal boys. The girls, Megan and Molly, made the sun shine on a rainy day. Both had been born with cerebral palsy, a disease causing partial paralysis of both legs, and wore ungainly ankle braces. Although Molly also needed a walker for additional support, she was already a pro at maneuvering around the classroom and hallways. In fact, Amy often had to remind Molly to slow down in the hallway. She loved to race! She and her sister were beautiful girls, with straight, honey-colored hair. When they smiled, their noses crunched up and their eyes twinkled. Whenever Amy thought of them, she felt happiness that threatened to overwhelm her. Molly and Megan made her glow. The fraternal boys, Joseph and Steven, were different from one another in appearance and personality. Handsome boys, one was timid and cautious, the other outspoken and fearless. Together with their elder sister, Elizabeth, Amy referred to them as "the ball of noise."

So many children touched Amy: children with learning disabilities, speech disorders and intellectual deficits, children from broken homes, kids who had been abused physically or emotionally, foster children, kids with attention deficit disorder (ADD) and attention deficit hyperactive disorder (ADHD.) They looked to Amy for educational guidance, support and positive reinforcement. They needed a pat on the back, a cheerful smile and a friendly, "You did a great job today."

In the second grade inclusion class, Amy helped children with behavioral and emotional problems or learning disabilities, along with regular students. The mixture of students made for a difficult classroom—the class was noisy and unruly at times—but Amy admired and respected the teacher, Mrs. Morgan, a dedicated woman who gave her finest professional qualities and instruction to that class. Amy worked in Mrs. Morgan's classroom at various times throughout the day, always learning something new and interesting, genuinely enjoying the instructor's deft handling of the different situations that arose.

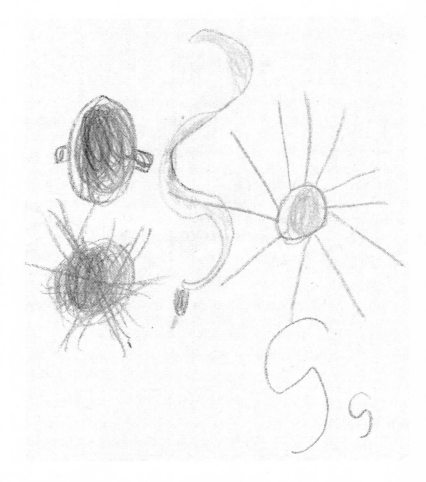

Mrs. Morgan was an inspiration to her, so Amy tried to give something back to this wonderful educator: Every day of that school year, Amy carefully wrote a small note of inspiration—a quote, a passage from Poor Richard's Almanac, a snippet from a motivational calendar—folded the note and handed it to Mrs. Morgan each morning. The sayings were pithy and familiar—"They who have nothing to be troubled at, will be troubled at nothing," "Lost time is never found again, "Early to bed and early to rise, makes a man healthy, wealthy and wise," "The doors of Wisdom are never shut"— not meant to be profound statements, but merely daily reminders that Mrs. Morgan's hard work was valued. When time allowed, Mrs. Morgan read the notes and smiled or laughed, appreciating each comment.

Amy was again expressing herself through her gift of writing, uncovering the kindness and generosity that had been locked inside her for so many years. She began to realize that she was an honest, genuine and compassionate woman; she was sincere and a good person. When a friend or acquaintance of hers experienced feelings of joy, accomplishment, sorrow or grief, Amy was able to write honest, open letters to them, just to let them know she was thinking of them. For the first time in her conscious memory, her positive side was beginning to become stronger than her negative side. When Amy's mother had been gone 18 months, Amy's monthly cycle returned, a good sign that her grief was subsiding. Her weight edged up ever so slightly, progressing above 90 lbs.; however, her grief for her mother-in-law was very fresh, and she knew her children were still sad that their grandmothers were gone. She had to hold herself together for them.

Toward the end of the 2000 school year, Amy's classes took their annual field trips. She had not been on a school bus since she was a student herself. She wanted to attend with the teachers and the students with whom she had worked with that year, but she was anxious about the experience. Then she remembered the subway ride in Philadelphia—if she could survive that adventure, then she could certainly ride a school bus! That is what she did, participating in two field trips, one with her son's first-grade class. She had surmounted another obstacle.

The class toured the Lackawanna Coal Mine, taking a train ride through the mine. After emerging from the dark mine into bright daylight, a young girl seated near Amy made an unsettling comment: "Look, look at the hair on Mrs. Bailey's face!" She pointed to Amy's face. "She looks like a werewolf!" Amy was mortified, but she could not show the young girl how bad she felt; Amy knew that young children often said things in a blunt, uninhibited manner that adults found too direct. Although Amy did not respond to the girl, she realized the growth of hair on her face had become visible to others.

All along Amy's jaw line and chin was a fine, soft covering of hair. Was it caused by age? Was it a premenopausal symptom? Was it because her body was in such a hormonal imbalance that the hair had begun to appear? She thought the latter must be true. Amy had read about this particular symptom with anorexic patients: lanugo. Her body was trying to protect itself from malnutrition—and the resulting low body temperatures—by growing this fine, downy-like hair. In some cases, fine hair could cover the entire body. If one little girl saw this lanugo, others did, too; the child had just been honest enough to say something. Amy could not hide the unsightly growth. She was embarrassed.

She sought the assistance of a woman who specialized in electrolysis, receiving the treatments bimonthly at first, and then weekly, until most of the hair was gone. She also made an appointment with her family physician, who prescribed a lotion that would inhibit further hair growth. The treatments and lotion were costly, but ridding herself of this problem was imperative. Not once did she consider the easiest way to remedy the problem: achieve a normal weight again.

Amy did become more aware of how her mind and body had deteriorated from the years of self-abuse. Did she want to continue living that way? She could not stop to confront her emotional state; she still feared a breakdown. She slogged forward, working the two jobs. Her legs ached from standing during the bakery shifts, her pace slowing as she climbed her stairs at home. She was fatigued and knew her blood pressure was low. However, her calorie intake and food consumption overruled any common sense she may have had about correcting her physical condition. She was constantly obsessed with the time, place and amount of food she ate; she became focused on halves of food. Half meant less eaten than the whole item; therefore it was lighter and less filling. The nighttime numbness in her bones worsened. Why was one half of her mind extremely positive, and the other so resistively negative?

In October of 2000, a significant opportunity became available for Amy within the school district: a full-time position as an enabler for a boy in junior high school. The applicant was required to follow junior high curriculum and exhibit knowledge of basic algebra. She submitted her letter of interest to the Superintendent, and a short time later, the Director of Special Education called Amy and told her she had the job. She was hesitant about accepting it, asking if she could first discuss the position with her husband.

She and James took into consideration many aspects of the new job: it would require a 20-minute drive to another school, the junior-high day began earlier and ended earlier than the elementary schedule, and they would need to adjust their pick-up and drop-off schedule for Shawn and Jim Jr. The few minor inconveniences were offset by the positive aspects of the job: an additional two-and-a-half hours of work meant increased income, but it also meant that Amy would be increased to full-time status, receiving health benefits, vision and dental care and prescription medication at a drastically reduced cost. She would also have more seniority, which would enable her to get even better jobs in the future. She accepted the job and began that November.

Amy had not realized the impression she had made on the elementary-school faculty. On her last day of work, the K-3 teachers presented her with a beautiful Bath & Body Works gift basket, filled with delightfully scented bath oils and lotions. Waiting for her in the office was a fresh, fall-hued floral arrangement from the entire faculty and staff. She was truly touched by their generosity and thoughtfulness, which made it all the more difficult for her to say good-bye. However, deep down, she knew the change would only lead to greater opportunities and a brighter future.

She hoped.

Joseph and the Library

She met Joseph on her first day at the vast Elementary/Middle School in the Valley. The special education teacher, Mr. Ross, explained Joseph's condition and gave Amy directives on his capabilities and behaviors: Joseph was autistic.

After the office secretary summoned him to Mr. Ross' classroom, she met Joseph for the first time. A strong and sturdy twelve-year-old boy with light-brown hair and glasses, Joseph cordially introduced himself as "Joey," said he was pleased to meet Amy, and then shook her hand, his eyes immediately darting away. Amy followed him back to his class; she would shadow him throughout the day, assisting him as needed.

With the exception of physical education, Amy pulled up a chair next to Joey in every class, concentrating on keeping him focused and on task. His curriculum contained all the regular-education junior high classes—language arts, pre-algebra, social studies and science—as well as his "specials"—art, gym, music, consumer and environmental sciences and foreign language. Even though he was autistic, the teachers did not adapt the quizzes or tests for him. He strictly followed all regular educational testing, as he and his parents had requested.

Amy and Joey quickly connected. She listened to him closely, learning how his mind functioned. She observed the way he processed oral and written material, noting that he read fluently and retained information when he prepared for quizzes and tests. At times, he needed prompting. He lacked social skills and became confused by oral directions; his auditory perception was deficient. His math skills, however, were exceptional. In addition to Amy's help, Joseph received private weekly math tutoring and special assistance preparing for exams and papers.

All students were responsible for keeping a homework assignment book, in which they logged instructions, homework assignments and information about extracurricular activities. Responsible for ensuring everything in Joey's book was properly recorded, Amy wrote notes to his parents about any difficulties he encountered throughout the day, as well as remarks about upcoming events, meetings or projects due; she also made a point to document Joey's positive achievements every day. Amy and Joey's mother Pat, kept in contact through the assignment book, and from time to time, she met with Amy at the school to discuss any problems or changes to Joseph's schedule. Amy had confidence in herself, which made his parents feel comfortable with their son's new aide. They knew Joey was in good hands. This was a first for Amy.

Intrigued by Joey's condition, Amy began to research autism. She needed to understand more about it. She looked in the library and online, finding a great deal of information on the National Institute of Mental Health's website. Autism was thought to be a brain disorder affecting a person's ability to communicate, form relationships with others and respond to his or her environment. Some people with autism were relatively high functioning, like Joseph, able to speak and reason intelligently. In some cases, people with more severe autism could seem closed off and shut down; still others seemed locked into repetitive behaviors and rigid patterns of thinking. Some were painfully sensitive to sound, touch, sight or smell. In most cases, autism first appears between 18 and 36 months of age; autistic children suddenly reject people, act strangely and lose language and social skills they had already acquired. Autism affected one or two people in every thousand, and is three to four times more common in boys than in girls. Although people with autism did not have exactly the same symptoms and deficits, they did tend to share certain social, communication, motor and sensory problems that affected their behavior in predictable ways.

Amy learned that children with autism often fixate on events, objects and places. Joey loved Disney films and spoke about his favorite characters constantly, often asking Amy about her favorites. He absolutely loved *The Lion King* and had seen it on Broadway in New York—as well as in Los Angeles—a total of 13 times. He had memorized all the characters' lines and often quoted them. But Amy was truly amazed when Joseph revealed his artistic talents. When he put his pencil to paper, he miraculously transferred his thoughts and visual retention onto paper. She really couldn't believe his ability—he'd draw characters from *The Lion King,* Disney movies and *The Wizard of Oz*, animals, scenes and portraits of his friends—even one of Amy.

He was mesmerized with Professional Wrestling—WWF *and* WCW. His favorite wrestler was The Rock. One day, he drew the faces of a dozen wrestlers. Amy, of course, did not know more than two or three of them, but when Joey showed his friends the picture, they put a name to each one of the twelve faces. He was so precise with his sketches. His artistic genius was untouchable! Amy often carried colored pencils in her tote bag so that Joey could color his drawings in intricate detail.

Several times over a given day, Joey exhibited particular hand motions and developed visual fixations on people or objects. Amy worked with him to keep his eyes focused and to redirect hand or head motions. It was a challenge for her, but Joey was a bright student and took his studies very seriously. He strove for perfection and studied intently. When Amy first worked with him, he became very upset with himself if he received a low grade on a quiz or test. He always said that his mother would get mad at him. With time, he adjusted; he would say to Amy, "Sometimes you get good grades, and sometimes you get bad grades." It was a big achievement for him.

Joey had a special notebook in which he planned his daily after-school activities, carefully numbering each item on his list. For example, he would write: 1. Play videogames after school; 2. Eat dinner; 3. Study for language arts test; 4. Take a shower; 5. Watch *Monday Night Raw Wrestling* on television; 6. Go to bed. He listed anything from six to twelve items each day. The following day, during his first-period class, he drew lines through each completed activity and composed a new list for the day. A ritual developed over years, these lists helped him keep his mind organized.

Although Joey had any number of methods for adapting to changing school requirements, Junior High brought something new: unexpected feelings for the young girls in his class. He had a crush on one special girl in the seventh grade. Somewhat fixated on her, he tried to get her attention after classes and became disturbed if he didn't have time to speak with her. If she was unresponsive, he became very upset. He shed more than one tear over the puppy love he felt for her. Even though Joey was autistic, he had many friends and was a popular young boy, waving at students in the hallways as classes changed. Everyone genuinely accepted him. He harbored a very close-knit group of friends, who had looked out for him for years: Mitchell, Ben, Jacob, Carmine, Chip, Elizabeth, Ashley and Valerie.

His parents loved Joey dearly and worked with him continuously, as did his various physicians, specialists and tutors, providing everything they could for Joseph and involving him with outside services available for children with autism. He had classes in social skills, etiquette and foreign language, and every Wednesday night, he and his parents attended a group that discussed treatment, coping skills, therapy and, perhaps, the hope for a cure for these special-needs children.

Amy quickly became attached to Joey. As she shadowed him each day, he began to grow on her, entering her heart and settling inside. He filled a large part of another empty chamber in her heart. His gaze sometimes seemed to flow directly through her, his eyes piercing, a trait of his disability. Joey looked to Amy for constant reassurance, praise and approval. His favorite sign was "thumbs up," which she gave for positive reinforcements, proper behavior and noteworthy accomplishments. Picking up on her fascination with his eyes, Joey became infatuated with winking at her. He occasionally complimented her on how pretty she was or how nice she looked. She concentrated on redirecting those types of behavior.

As Amy worked full time, her days became active and occupied, leaving her less time for her home and family. She bottled in the guilt that stabbed at her, worrying about Shawn's change in routine and how he was handling it. When Amy got home, it was around 3:00 P.M. She barely had time to change clothing, greet Abbey, wave at Jim as he came home from high school, and then run out the door to pick up Shawn from school. In the evenings were filled with homework and studying, basketball practice, dinner, showers, television and bedtime. When the school year ended, Amy was assigned as Joey's enabler for the eighth grade. She was delighted, but she worried about the impact on her time with her family.

She knew it was time to end her employment at Wal-Mart. Because she was so much busier with Joey than she had been as a part-time aide, working two jobs was becoming unhealthy for her physical and emotional state. After she resigned, she found she had too much free time to think; she needed some diversion from her grief and unhappiness. Her priorities in turmoil, she registered for a computer course at her local community college, a class that ran for three months on Sunday mornings, 8:00 A.M.-11:00 A.M. It was almost more than she could manage, but she craved the additional stress and pressure. It kept her from feeling pain. Amy allotted time to study and complete computer assignments. She badgered herself relentlessly, but she rationalized that if she had a better knowledge of computer skills and technology, it would benefit her when other positions became available. It was a difficult road, but she completed the course with a B grade. Of course, she was upset that it wasn't an A, but she had tried the best she could.

As the summer of 2001 approached, Amy feared unstructured time—three months of it. It was too much time to dwell on the past. She refused to feel the pain. What could she do to occupy herself? Her local library came to mind. Each summer brought a new theme for the children's reading program, incorporating activities and coordinating the reading theme throughout June, July and August. Young Jim—and now Shawn—always participated in the program. Perhaps Amy could volunteer a few hours at the library. She spoke with the branch librarian about the possibility and found that they were looking for a part-time person to work 15 hours a week. She suggested Amy apply for the summer job and be placed on the payroll. Amy applied and was hired.

Fifteen hours a week was perfect. Shawn had three cousins in town whom he alternated visiting on Amy's workdays. He enjoyed the time he spent with them. Young Jim had a part-time job at a local supermarket. He turned sixteen and immediately went for his driver's permit. An agreeable schedule, the summer seemed to work out for everyone.

Amy discovered a new field of interest. She was eager to learn library skills and book shelving in accordance with the Dewey Decimal System, to give input on the children's crafts and to stress the importance of reading for pleasure. Most of the children that participated in the summer reading program were students she knew from Shawn's elementary school. It was gratifying to see them again. She chatted with the kids and their parents, as well as various other members of the community, who regularly checked out books. Both a quiet zone and a social one, Amy loved both aspects of the library. Working there, she realized she was good at something else;

discovering her aptitude for this work was almost like opening a new book for the first time.

Summertime was always less stressful. There were no deadlines, no dates, no homework and no schedules to follow. In mid-August, when the program ended, the library held a party for all the children. The librarian, knowing of Amy's cake-decorating skills, asked if she would bake and decorate two sheet cakes for the celebration. The party was a success, and Amy hoped to work there again the following summer.

There were two weeks of summer remaining. The family took their vacation to Canada, and also spent a weekend at Jim's sister's farmhouse in late August. Each week that summer, Amy telephoned the administrative-office secretary, Janice, and asked if any new postings were available in the district; Janice would read all the new positions to her. Amy loved helping Joey, but she had to find something closer to home. As the school year approached, she became anxious about returning to work. She was looking forward to seeing Joey again, but she still felt so far away from Shawn. She felt like the job was tearing her apart. She sensed a breakdown was near. Consumed with torment, tired of the struggle, she felt as if she just couldn't tolerate the lifelong battle for one more day. This was not her fault! After one prolonged session of journal writing, Amy stood up, picked up the telephone, called her doctor and asked her to start her on Prozac again. She could not endure this without assistance In September; she began to take 20mg of Prozac daily and was scheduled to see her doctor every three months. With her full-time employment and benefit plan, the fee for the antidepressants was only five dollars. Her job was such a blessing in disguise! She could finally afford to take the antidepressant that had always succeeded in stabilizing her. Perhaps things would be different now, finally.

Young Jim was a junior in high school, Shawn was in third grade, and Joey was in his final year of junior high. Each day, Amy drove Jim Jr. to the bus stop, and James took Shawn to school before continuing on to work. Amy hesitantly departed for the Valley School, feeling confident that her medication would soon relieve her anxiety.

Joseph's first class of the day was language arts. As Amy entered the classroom, Joseph sat in the last row, in the last seat next to the windows. He lifted his head, glanced at Amy as she walked toward him and gave her a timid smile. They talked a little about his summer, and his friends gazed her way and gave a welcoming smile—Carmen, Jacob, Ben and Mitch. After class, Joey told Amy about all the places he had visited over the summer. He gathered with his friends, and then they were off to music class. His schedule consisted of Algebra I, science, social studies and an introduction to French and Spanish. Amy was looking forward to the language class. At the day's end, they always departed five minutes earlier than the bell rang, which gave Joey ample time to get to his locker and gather his belongings and homework for the evening. Amy walked outside with him every day, waiting with him until his mother or another family member arrived.

According to Amy's union contract, in her school district, an aide was allowed to change positions once during a new school year. Periodically, she glanced at the job postings in the school office. She knew another placement would come her way. Because she liked Joey so much, she felt guilty as she scanned the bulletin board. She assumed the office staff watched her as she searched for a new job. Her insecurity must have flashed like fireworks.

Trauma and heartache hit our world on September 11, 2001, for some more than others. Amy sat next to Joey in his third-period Algebra I class, watching the television reports; Joey's teacher, Mr. Snyder, had turned on the overhead television. The entire class was fixated as everyone viewed the tragedy, sitting in awe and disbelief as the tragedy unfolded before their eyes. Joseph sat, pencil in hand, and wrote his numbered list of his after-school plans for that day. Amy wanted to shelter him from the horror, for she was uncertain of his reaction or comprehension of it.

Sara, a young girl who sat to Amy's right, became upset, fearing for her safety. Soon, the other students began to ask questions. Amy stood up and approached Mr. Snyder, quietly whispering to him about the students' distress. He turned off the television and spoke calmly and reassuringly to them. Those who had questions and concerns comfortably spoke aloud to the class. Joseph continued to write until the class period ended. He spoke not a word of that early-morning incident until they walked out of the building at dismissal. He said, "Mrs. Bailey, what happened at the Trade Center, that was bad." He had heard and understood everything that had happened, but his reaction was particular to his autism.

As it happened, Joey's parents had been planning to go to New York on September 11, but had to cancel the trip to attend a co-worker's funeral service. Had they gone on the trip, they would have dined at the World Trade Center that same night.

Soon after that, the first marking period drew to an end. It was a week full of exams, studies, tutoring and concentration for Joey. During the week of quarterly exams, Amy once again checked the office postings. To her surprise, she saw a library aide position had become available at a recently built elementary/middle school, which was closer to her home. A five-hour-a-day position, it was considered full-time, so she would keep her benefits. The only drawback was a decrease in salary, but the school's closer proximity might be worth it. She delivered a letter of interest to the superintendent, noting her recent library experience and recently acquired computer skills.

Joey's exams ended on a Thursday. That morning, Amy received a message to telephone the superintendent. On her lunch break, she called and found she had been offered the library aide position. Her first day of work would begin on Monday. She had until the end of the day to make her decision.

Amy called Jim at work immediately. They discussed the drawbacks and advantages of the new job, uncertain about what to do. The real problem was the decrease in pay. Could they afford the job change? It was impossible to have a discussion and resolve the matter over the telephone; Jim and Amy needed to make the final decision at home. Amy called the superintendent and asked if she could have until the morning to respond. Her request was granted.

With the guidance and support of James, his aunt and cousin, and Amy's sister, Ann, they deliberated, weighed the pros and cons and finally decided. Amy accepted the position. The hours and distance were shorter, and after reviewing their budget, they found they could manage very well with the change in salary. She, James and Shawn would be able to leave their home at the same time in the morning.

Her new job requirements involved assisting the school librarian with grades four through six. Students in kindergarten through third grade would be solely Amy's responsibility. She would help the children select their library books for that week, check out the books and generally keep the kids structured and focused through class, reading them a story toward the end of the period. She would begin her day at 8:30 A.M., reporting each day to the cafeteria. She would monitor the incoming students who had breakfast at school and the other students as they arrived for the day. She would also monitor a few lunch periods, as well. Her day would end at 1:30 P.M., which allowed ample time for household responsibilities or shopping before she picked up Shawn after school. For such a perfect schedule, she and James certainly could sacrifice a few extra dollars. Amy was so excited about working with elementary students again!

Early Friday morning, Amy called to report in a sick day and request a substitute for Joey. She had not slept a wink all night. She then made the telephone call and accepted the position, promising that she'd begin on Monday. She drove to Valley, gathered her belongings and bade farewell to the wonderful group of teachers and aides with whom she'd had the pleasure of working. Some how, some way, she'd explain to Joey that she would no longer be able to work with him. When Amy thought of that discussion, her excitement turned to sadness, but deep down she knew that when she saw him, the right words would come to her.

Amy spoke to Joey after lunch, during Social Studies. Since exams were over, the class had been viewing a movie. Amy took Joey into the hallway and explained to him simply that another job had become available for her. It was closer to her home, and she would begin on Monday. A new person would be there to work with him that day. She took his hands and wished him well. Joey listened, but Amy was not certain whether or not he understood her. When she was finished, he simply said, "Thank you, Mrs. Bailey. You have a nice day," and returned to class. Amy moved into the stairwell and began to cry. She exited the building, feeling unsettled. She needed to telephone his mother and explain the circumstances to her. She knew it would not be an easy task.

On her way home, Amy stopped at her new school and familiarized herself with her new surroundings. She spoke with the office staff, and they directed her to the library. The principal met with her there and gave her a tour of the building. She would meet with the librarian on Monday and begin her new responsibilities. Everyone Amy met that day welcomed her warmly and assured her that she'd love the school and the new job. As she drove home, she felt very content and confident that she had made the right decision.

Joseph's mother was indeed upset when she first heard from Amy. Pat said that Amy had a very positive connection with Joey and had been helping him make excellent progress in junior high. She was very sorry to lose Amy, but she did understand that a new opportunity awaited her. Because many aides had worked with her son throughout his school years, his mother had taken him through these changes before. Pat said she would miss Amy and genuinely wished her good luck in the library.

After Pat said good-bye, Joey took the telephone. Amy explained herself in a manner that was more comfortable for both of them. She promised to stop by his school to see him, and said they could talk on the phone. He said that would be a good idea. She told him that his new aide would work very well with him, because he was a very special student. After they said good-bye, she felt more at ease.

Joey would always do well; he was an exceptional and very special boy. He would be guided properly and well provided for in his future years, whether or not Amy was by his side. Later, whenever Amy thought of Joey, memories of him permeated her soul. Words could not describe his presence in her heart; he certainly nestled within a special place in it.

Her Place and Her Peace

First days at a new job always involve nervous jitters, apprehension and new challenges, but Amy was happy and eager to work with elementary children again. In the library, she had three to four classes on a daily basis. She met many new faces: faculty, staff, maintenance workers, cafeteria women, PTA volunteers—and the children, of course! From breakfast duty, to the library, to lunchroom monitoring, Amy blended well with it all. She met the librarian, Mrs. Thomas, a tall, slender, dark-haired woman in her 50s, who had a charming personality. She made Amy feel at ease. Amy adjusted to her new routine in the very first week. She felt comfortable, confident and in control.

It was early November. She had been on the anti-depressant for two months. Something was different this time, definitely different. She felt likable, even lovable. She was positive and focused, full of ideas for the children in the library. She played cards with the breakfast crew in the morning, and they connected, talked and laughed. The kids were eager to see her each day; she saw and complimented their school projects, discovered their likes and dislikes and, occasionally, disciplined the more rowdy children. When the second bell rang, the students went off to their homerooms and started their day. She felt bubbly and had the bounce back in her step.

Watching the young ones each day, she was reminded how individual and unique each child was, with innocent smiles, twinkling eyes, missing teeth, slicked hair, spiked hair, ponytails and braids, quiet and shy, talkative and squirmy, helpful, mannerly, attentive, eager, impressionable and lovable—children. She saw the kids who

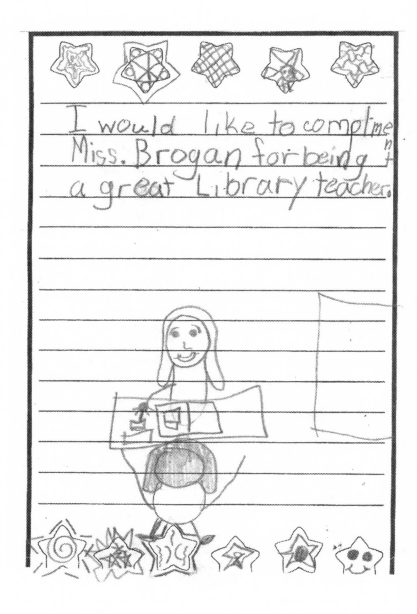

I would like to compolme Miss. Brogan for being a great Library teacher.

yearned for attention, who lacked the ability to ask for help, who were abused physically, emotionally and verbally, children with special needs, those who were neglected and children who just needed a little tender loving care and a kind and trusting person to listen to them. These kids gave so much of themselves to Amy. One by one, they stepped inside her, like Joey had done, and took their distinctive place. In return, Amy discovered that she had so much to give back, so much to offer to them.

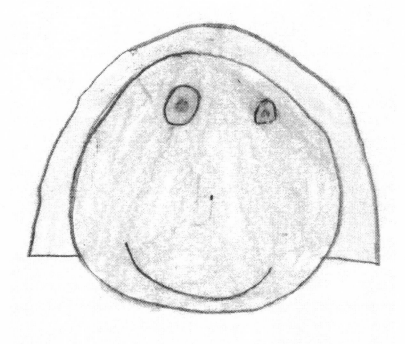

Mrs. Brogan

Amy had such a surge of energy. Her thoughts were in constant motion. The new library held hundreds of books; however, it lacked an atmosphere of warmth and welcome. Once Amy stepped in, the reading corner soon flourished with dozens of adorable, cuddly critters. Amy searched her attic at home, and she and her boys donated their old stuffed animals, which completely filled the tops of four bookshelves. They became the "library friends" and listened to every story. She made bookmarks and decorations. She filled a large, colorful, empty cookie tin with prizes she gave out to the children on their birthdays. She handed out stickers and lollipops and treats on special occasions. If time allowed, she involved the children in small projects and activities. On holidays, students drew and colored pictures to highlight the library bulletin board. They crafted Christmas cards, Valentines, shamrocks and Easter décor. The children took turns and read to their class, with Amy asking questions about the story, assessing their comprehension. Occasionally, the children watched an episode of *Reading Rainbow* episode or another short video. As Amy drove home after school each day, she'd call James on her cell phone, just to tell him how happy she was and how much she loved her work in the library. Her thoughts grew positive with each new day, which placed her focus on food and weight less imperative. She climbed toward 100 lbs.

Toward the end of the school year, the school principal evaluated all the aides. Amy had never had an evaluation before, and she was nervous, riddled with uncertainty. She needn't have worried—her evaluation was exceptional! Each comment and observation was very positive, showing little need for improvement. Amy was astounded. She was proud and pleased with herself—she could make a difference. This was her place. She had finally found it.

Amy had the best of everything that anyone could have hoped for: a loving husband of twenty-four years, two sons, her faithful companion, Abbey, a beautiful home and a fulfilling job, where she felt like Mother Goose each time she gathered the children to read to them. She also had the peacefulness of the quiet library setting. Her eyes had finally opened. There was sunshine over her head. She hugged her kids and gave much-needed attention to her girl, Abbey. She laughed, joked and played pranks with her boys. As for her husband, she felt like she had on their first date together, head-over-heels in love with him, all over again. James definitely noticed the difference, saying to Amy one day that he was so glad she was back. She was living again. She was a happy, loving and giving person. Most important, she had accepted herself for whom she was, and she loved herself as much as she loved those held close inside her heart.

Now that her first year was over, Amy and the boys had three full months off. She spent every day with them. She had no summer job and rarely made the time for volunteer work. She was just too busy loving her kids. The only other activity she pursued was her writing, which she began again in May. She never imagined she had so much to say. Six months later, everything she had held inside was finally on paper.

Amy's mother had been gone for five years. Only after Amy wrote her story was she able to look at photographs of her mother and speak of her in the past tense. It was the first August she could change her calendar blocks on the top of her microwave oven from 21 to 22 without pain, accepting the date for what it was: the anniversary of her mother's death. Amy snipped a bouquet of black-eyed susans from her flowerpots, tied them together and placed them near her mother's headstone. Her mother had loved flowers, especially black-eyed susans, which always grew in a remote corner of her garden. Amy was grateful her sons had had the chance to know their grandmothers.

At the end of their summer vacation, Amy and her sons began a major project: They attacked the attic, anticipating a huge garage sale in late September. The time had come for a major overhaul. Like Amy's once-bottled-up memories and emotions, so much had been stored in that attic for so long. There was barely enough room to get around. They tackled a new section each day, boxing and bagging, tossing out and tagging toys and games, clothing, coats, chairs and table, seasonal items and other items they had rarely, if ever, used. They came to a section where Amy had stored newspaper-wrapped pictures, next to an antique cherry dresser that Amy's father had refinished for them. Wedged in between was a six-foot-long piece of rolled brown mailing paper. Young Jim carefully unraveled it. Amy glanced at it and gasped, not realizing she had saved it. Young Jim wanted to know what it was, so they unrolled the life-sized tracing of their mother's body, made when she was at the Graduate Eating Disorder Unit in Philadelphia, back in 1990. In the upper-right-hand corner, the date read 12-14-90. Below that was written "96 lbs." In the center of the gaunt, emaciated body tracing were the phrases

"Take care of your body" and "Ask for help and support." In the left-hand corner were the words "Ghostly, white invisible image, in

another world." Amy remembered when she had laid on that piece of brown paper while the art therapist traced her body with a pencil. Amy highlighted the pencil line with a black marker and then wrote those words, explaining what that image had meant to her on that day in December.

Now, 12 years later, she stood with her boys and looked at that tracing. To her sons, her time in the Graduate Hospital was a hidden part of her life. Amy rarely spoke of it, and Shawn was completely unaware his mother had ever been hospitalized. Little Jim had only been five in 1990. She remembered how she and her husband had described her condition to Jim. Following her therapist's suggestion, they had explained to Jim why his mother could not eat. They had said that his mom was so filled with sadness and uncomfortable feelings that she had very little room left inside her body for food. She needed to release and let go of those feelings. Only then would she have room inside her body and soul for nutrition.

As she and her boys gazed the image, Amy explained to them what the picture represented and why it had been made. Young Jim sadly whispered, "Mom, you were only 96 lbs."

She explained that 96 pounds was an improvement on her condition when she entered the hospital, when she weighed only 90 lbs. "I am no longer there, boys," she said, confident she was telling the truth.

Jim's head lowered as he spoke, "Don't ever do that to me again, Mommy."

Amy's heart sunk, feeling his pain. "It will never happen again," she promised. She embraced the two of them. "Let's fold this up and throw it in the trash," she said. "We don't need this." In a few moments, the picture was gone, and with it, the person she used to be.

Amy learned from her experiences in therapy that emotions

needed to be expressed, the good and the bad. That was positively true for one's emotional well being and stability. Not one person is perfect. Everyone is on this earth together. Amy taught her children to express themselves, to do what felt right for them and to try their best at everything they encountered. She taught them that it is all right to ask for help when they needed it. Amy was an honest, giving and loving person. She embraced herself in those three simple, kind words.

Amy celebrated her 45th birthday in January of 2003. She was 45 and alive and stronger and happier than she had ever been before. Not long after that, James asked her if she'd ever determined the source of her problems. "Did you ever really figure it out?"

"Yes, Jim," was her answer. She showed him her journals, her recorded thoughts and feelings during the darkest time in her life. "The answers are here, in all of these pages."

She had found all the pieces of her puzzling life and placed them together into a large, wonderful picture. She had transformed her missing pieces into "peace."

In the End

This is to address all the individuals that suffer from, or suspect they suffer from, the disorder known as anorexia nervosa. Understand that you are not alone in your struggle with food. Anorexia is an illness, a disorder, and it is not your fault. You may think that you are in control and that control makes you feel important, worthwhile and useful. The truth is that this demeaning, debilitating disorder has the ultimate control over *you*. It will take you down deeper and deeper into despair and hopelessness.

Find the hidden strength that lies within you. It is present; ask someone for help and pull your self to the surface. You cannot do it alone. Reach out to a sibling, a parent, a friend or a teacher. All you need is one person to listen to you.

Anorexia is not caused by one simple factor. If it were, Amy would have finished writing her story on only one page. Anorexia is a very complicated disease. Only after writing everything out was Amy able to discover the intricate details of life. Figuring out the sources of anorexia takes time, therapy, medication, patience and love and support from family and friends. Excellent, qualified therapists are available, skillfully trained professionals, especially in eating disorder therapy. In addition to these specialists, acute medical care units and outpatient therapy services are available to help you. Seek them out.

You are a unique and important individual. There is no one else exactly like you. You deserve the best in life. You are a special person. You do matter. Amy has been there. She does understand. She cares about you. Many others do as well. Find those people and take their hands. They will help you and bring you back among the living. Recovery is a sometimes-lengthy process. Take it one step at a time, one day at a time. Amy is recovering, and so can you!

When the time came for Amy and her siblings to take on the task of looking through their mother's estate and personal belongings, Amy stumbled upon a poem her mother had written when she was a young woman. She had signed the poem with her maiden name, which meant she had been about 19 or 20 at the time. Amy knew her mother had written many memoirs, but they only found this one poem:

A Perfect Day

I love to smell the fragrances of the rose and lily white,
To walk among the gardens, when the day is clear and bright.
I love to watch the insects, as they crawl along the walk,
And watch the little toad, when he sits upon a rock.

I love to feel the breeze as it ruffles through my hair,
Especially on a hilltop, where it's much cooler there.
I love to lie and watch the clouds, as they go rolling by,
So picturesque, as they are placed against the clear, blue sky.

I love to hear the bluebirds and the robins when they sing;
Their tone is so cheerful, that you surely know it's spring.
I love to watch the sunset, as it shows the end of day,
As all the little children run, to put their toys away.

I love to watch the twilight, the nicest time of all,
The stars twinkle in and out and purple shadows fall.
The moon beams ever brightly and shows you on your way,
Down from the rolling hill, to end this perfect day.

D.K.

A perfect ending to an imperfect creation.

Anorexia Nervosa

"Anorexia nervosa is a psychiatric disorder characterized by self-induced weight loss. An individual's weight drops to 85% or less of ideal body weight. 100 pounds is considered a normal amount for a woman five feet tall. Add five pounds more for each additional inch of weight; plus or minus 10% of that figure would be a normal weight range. A person loses weight by severe dietary restriction, over-exercising or purging (meaning self-induced vomiting and/or laxative abuse).

"Individuals with anorexia have a tremendous fear of eating and feel as though their appetite and weight will go out of control. They have a distorted body image, meaning they do not see how thin they are and insist that they are too fat.

"Outright denial of the illness is very common. Anorectics do not see how thin they are and feel that they are not in any danger, showing resentment to friends and family who try to help them. The disorder is most frequently seen in young women. Around five to seven percent of patients are male, and age range can be from preteen to late middle age.

"Underlying emotional factors and problems debilitate the people with this disorder. Self-induced starvation is the way to resolve complex inner struggles and conflicts. Problems may involve the individual's family, assuming adult responsibilities, abuse or dealing with sexuality. There is usually a very negative sense of self-worth and self-esteem and feelings of unworthiness. Control becomes the main issue. The anorectic individual substitutes the control over her food and weight for the control over her life. Most people on a diet stop at their goal weight or simply give up on it before reaching it. The person with an eating disorder reaches her goal, and then continues. This grants her the feeling of mastery and accomplishment. Each time the numbers on the scale drop lower, a new goal is set: 120 pounds, 110 pounds, 95 pounds and so on. There is always a new goal to set or a goal to maintain.

"Slow starvation and nutritional deficiencies usually brings on depression. There may also be a genetic link between anorexia and depression, as depression is often seen in the families of anorectic patients. In this dangerous and critical state of depression, suicidal tendencies may arise.

"Medical complications soon begin to occur. In acute stages, dehydration and blood chemical imbalances result in low blood pressure and heart arrhythmias. With weight down to near 60 percent ideal body weight, serious complications arise, including heart failure, kidney failure and overwhelming infections. Long term, or chronic complications, which develop over several years, includes osteoporosis (loss of calcium in the bones), possible loss of fertility, circulatory problems and loss of kidney function.

"Time, years of time, in some cases, is totally wasted. While peers are completing their education, starting careers, finding relationships and starting families, the anorectic is stuck in their obsessive behaviors of dieting and weight control. If the problem has persisted for several years, the individual has much more difficulty in settling back into a lifestyle with her peers, and will discover the same, if not more, difficulty, in overcoming anorexia."

A Note from the Author

Inside Amy is a true story of my life. I am not a distinguished, prominent, recognized author of our time. I am a mother, a wife, a sister, an aunt, a godmother and a friend, a woman who suffered silently from verbal abuse as a child, and later in life, became a victim of anorexia nervosa. Although many books discuss eating disorders from different points of view, my book is distinct because it recounts my personal experience as a mother with anorexia nervosa. Throughout the book, I refer to myself as Amy, a name I always loved from childhood.

I was compelled to write this book as a form of therapy, a way to obtain my own sense of inner peace. I never imagined how many years of unspoken emotions I had to release on paper. Once I had finished writing my story, I realized that I needed others to read it; I wanted to help the hundreds and thousands of those who are afflicted with eating disorders or have been victims of abuse. Within these pages, I have learned to accept myself for the beautiful person I have become and found the courage to say, "I survived." I want to reach out to all ages, inform them to seek outside sources and realize it is acceptable to ask for help.